Quercus Editions Ltd
55 Baker Street
7th Floor, South Block
London
W1U 8EW

First published in 2014

A CIP catalogue record for this book is available from the British Library

ISBN 978 1 84866 281 0
Printed and bound in Great Britain by Clays Ltd, St Ives Plc

10 9 8 7 6 5 4 3 2 1

Designed for Quercus Editions Ltd by Peggy Sadler at Bookworx
www.bookworx.biz

Contents

A note from the authors 4
Introduction 6

Chapter 1 The Low-Down on Mood 10

Chapter 2 Cognitive Behavioural Therapy 26

Chapter 3 Changing Your Behaviour 40

Chapter 4 Making Time for Yourself 54

Chapter 5 Physical Education 66

Chapter 6 Emotion Overload 82

Chapter 7 Mind Games 92

Chapter 8 Who Do You Think You Are? 110

Chapter 9 Taking Charge of Your Thoughts 126

Chapter 10 The *Real* Meaning of Life 138

A final message 147

Further reading 152
Useful websites 153
Acknowledgements 154

A Note From the Authors

We live in ever-changing times and sometimes life can be tough. We're constantly being pulled in different directions and can struggle to cope with the pressure that we're put under by external factors and, most importantly, by ourselves. With greater choice comes greater responsibility and occasionally this can be a breeding ground for stress, unhappiness and self-doubt. There are very few people (if any at all) who feel they operate perfectly in their work, relationships and life in general. Most of us could use some help now and then – a nudge to show us how to improve our mood, to change our approach to life and to feel more content.

This series aims to help you understand why you feel, think and behave the way you do – and then gives you the tools to make positive changes. We're not fans of complicated medical jargon so we've tried to make everything accessible, relevant and entertaining as we know you'll want to see improvements as soon as possible. These concise, practical guides show you how to focus your thinking, develop coping strategies and learn practical techniques to face anything and everything in more positive and helpful ways.

We believe self-help doesn't have to be confusing, worthy or patronising. We draw on our professional experience and the latest research, using anecdotes and examples which we found helpful and hope you will too. Titles are split into particular areas of concern such as sleep, happiness, confidence and stress, so you can focus on the areas you'd most like to address.

Our books are based on a Cognitive Behavioural Therapy (CBT) framework. CBT is an incredibly successful treatment for a wide variety of issues and we're convinced it will enable you to cope with whatever you're facing.

Within the books you'll regularly come across diagrams called mind maps. They are easy to use and simple to understand. Based on CBT, mind maps show how your thoughts, behaviour and how you feel (both emotionally and physically) are all connected, breaking the problem down so it doesn't seem overwhelming, and laying out options for making changes.

There are exercises and checklists throughout, to guide you through the practical steps of altering how you feel. We'll make it easy to make these changes part of your routine because reading the theory is only going to get you so far. The only way to ensure you'll feel better long-term is to put everything you learn into practice and change how you experience your day-to-day life.

You can *choose* to feel better and these books will show you how.

Good luck! Let us know how you get on by contacting us on our website: www.jessamyandjo.com

Jessamy and Jo

Introduction

Hello there. How are you? Good? Yep, us too. Isn't it wonderful how everyone's always fine, good or even great? It makes everything seem so nice and normal. Except feeling permanently fine isn't normal. Our ability to experience and process a range of thoughts and emotions is what makes us human, but unfortunately those thoughts and feelings can often be pretty dark. In reality everyone feels rubbish sometimes. Life can trip you up anytime it fancies, blindsiding you with dramas and dilemmas that can make you feel low, sad and depressed.

But don't panic, there's good news too …

Firstly, you *can* feel happier. There are strategies and tools contained within this book that will help you change negative thoughts, feelings and behaviour. If you're truly willing to invest a bit of time on yourself then you can completely change your life – and we're not just saying that. Keep reading – we're confident we'll convince you.

Secondly, you're not alone. Low mood is a common mental health problem and one in four people in the UK will experience some kind of mental health issue in the course of a year. Put another way, 25 per cent of people living in the UK have sought medical advice for concerns about their emotional well-being. While this stat won't prompt anyone to crack open the bubbly, it should be reassuring to know that at least some of the shiny happy people surrounding you might not be quite as shiny and happy as they make out. As far as feeling unhappy is concerned you're totally and utterly normal.

And thirdly, people generally don't sprint in the opposite direction when the phrase 'mental health' is mentioned any more – the stigma surrounding depression and feeling low is disappearing. Unfortunately, it does still exist in some areas, but in recent years there has been a dramatic increase in people's awareness of emotional health issues. Celebrity sufferers, such as Stephen Fry and Catherine Zeta Jones, now speak openly about their experiences of depression. There are countless campaigns from mental health charities, television programmes and magazines which all raise awareness. It is becoming as common for someone to want to look after their emotional health as it is for them to resolve any problems with their physical health – which is where this book comes in.

So why has unhappiness picked on you?

Feeling low happens to different people at different times for different reasons. You may have experienced a catastrophic life event, received some terrible news or be having a delayed response to something that happened a long time ago. Alternatively, feeling down may be your default state of mind – you're a glass half empty kind of person. You feel dissatisfied and disillusioned with life and with your situation. Or you may just be having a bad day, week or month. This happens to all of us sometimes and understanding why can help you to manage those moments and feel happier.

Sadness can become a crutch – a justification for avoiding real life. You feel so lonely and down that you're absolutely and 100 per cent convinced that something is inherently wrong with the way you were built. The 'having it all' and perfectionist culture we live in can make us feel guilty for feeling sad – as if it's somehow an admission of failure. Which is why we're glad you're reading this book! Things can get better and they will.

Who we are and what this book is about

Depression and sadness is a subject very close to our hearts. We have both experienced depression amongst our friends and families and believe that a book such as this could really have helped. We use the terms low mood, sad, feeling down and depression interchangeably because we believe the strategies we use will help you to feel better regardless of how long you've been feeling this way. We want to give practical and effective advice in a meaningful and accessible way. If you've been feeling monumentally crappy for a very long time please do try our suggestions, but also visit your GP and get things checked out in case you need more specialist help.

We believe looking after your emotional health is an integral part of having a good life. It's bizarre how most people think it's totally normal and natural to look after their physical health, going to the gym, eating healthily etc., but as soon as there's a whisper about paying attention to mental health people become suspicious and fearful as if caring about how your mind works is a bit weird. It couldn't be less weird – it's absolutely essential for feeling happy and for enjoying your life.

How the book works

This is a really practical book. We are determined to make a difference to your life and to help you feel happier. It's important that you become really familiar with every chapter and absorb the necessary information and skills as you go along. Each chapter builds on the next so we recommend that you read them in numerical order rather than jumping around, so stuff makes more sense. There's a method to the madness: the strategies at the beginning are simpler than the ones at the end. We adhere to the whole not running before you can walk shtick – doing things in order will be easier for you.

This is a manual, guiding you through what you need to do to feel happier, why you need to do it, and then reviewing each step. You need to give it the time it deserves. Don't get us wrong – a lot of these techniques will produce immediate results, but practising is what will ensure it becomes second nature. Take the strategies on board, practice them and then integrate them into your daily life; we're certain you'll feel happier.

How to get the most out of this book

+ Try all the strategies out rather than just skimming over them. These techniques are proven to work. Some may suit you better than others, but by trying them all you'll give yourself the best possible shot at feeling happier. The strategies are identified by this symbol **S**.
+ Breaking bad habits and adopting new positive ones takes a while (twenty-one days according to most experts) so you'll have to practise and repeat the strategies to encourage a lasting effect.
+ Buy a new notebook and dedicate it to this book. Several of our strategies involve or drawing stuff out. It'll be motivational to be able to flip back to what you've written and see how far you've come. Also, the very act of writing things down aids memory and will make your determination to change more 'official' in your head.

We believe depression, sadness and low mood are beatable. It's not something you have to just accept and live with forever. You can take back control of your life. Just wanting to make a change is a huge step and something to be proud of.

1

The Low-Down on Mood

Low mood can hugely affect your life. Here we explain what it is, where it might have come from and why it's got its claws into you. Understanding the whys and hows of unhappiness is an essential part of feeling better.

Why do we feel low?

Everyone feels sad, unhappy or low sometimes – and that's not even a bad thing. You can't know what it is to feel joy if you've never felt sorrow. You wouldn't be human if you didn't experience a range of emotions.

Mood naturally fluctuates. Picture a line with 'ridiculously happy' at one end and 'depressed' at the other. We slide up and down this line all the time depending on what's going on in our lives. It's all about balance. However, if you find yourself stuck down the unhappy end of the line for a while, then it's time to start asking questions. Once you're in a slump it can feel impossible to snap out of it and your bad day can turn into a bad week, month or year. But no matter how long you've been feeling grim, you can turn things around. There's no reason why you have to accept your mood as a permanent fixture. Once you understand why and how you feel the way you do, you'll be in a much better position to change it. Accepting that you do feel bad and that you want to feel better is a big deal. Recognising yourself in the explanations given opposite might also feel like a relief, a confirmation that you're not alone and that other people with similar experiences have come out the other side.

Depression, in all its many guises, is old. Ancient, in fact. Discussions of its origins usually start with the Greek physician, Hippocrates, who wrote, 'prolonged fear and sadness means melancholia', specifying that sufferers will have 'an aversion to food, sleeplessness, irritability and restlessness'. This diagnosis still stands up to scrutiny today and the symptoms Hippocrates and his disciples identified are as relevant now as they were in 400BC.

We all have the capability to feel sad, but some people are more predisposed to feel unhappy than others. It's something that can creep up on you out of nowhere, or stem from a specific event or trauma that can trigger more long-term feelings of melancholy. Depression doesn't only affect how we feel emotionally, but also how we think, behave and feel physically.

Clinical manuals characterise depression as a disorder that represents an alteration from previous 'functioning', such as a distinct change (for the worst) in how you're behaving and feeling. Sufferers will be experiencing five or more of the following symptoms during a two-week period (one of which must be low mood or diminished interest or pleasure):

+ Low mood
+ Diminished interest or pleasure
+ Change to appetite
+ Lack of sleep
+ Purposeless motions like pacing, wringing your hands or excessive fidgeting
+ Fatigue or loss of energy
+ Feelings of worthlessness or excessive/inappropriate guilt
+ Diminished ability to think or concentrate
+ Recurrent thoughts of death or suicide

The symptoms will be causing significant distress and impairment in social situations, work and other areas of your life. (It's important to rule out other causes, for example: mind-altering substances or a general medical condition.)

A note on bereavement

Some of these symptoms can be directly attributable to grief, which is a very different beast. While grief can lead to depression it is not the same thing; there are specific treatment methods dedicated to dealing with bereavement. If you have lost someone you love and recognise the above symptoms then please don't despair and/or disregard this book! We are dealing with low mood and depression rather than grief, but there will be techniques and strategies in here that can help you.

Barriers to seeking help

Women are far more likely to seek help for low mood than men. Perhaps this is in part due to men suffering from the embedded societal illusion that admitting something is wrong will be seen as a form of weakness. Maybe they believe that there's something slightly embarrassing in not just being able to 'man up' and get over it. Or perhaps it's because society has for years viewed mental health problems as something to be hidden. If it's not a physical problem – if you can't see it or fix it with surgery – it's somehow not 'real' and is therefore shameful. There is an inherent guilt linked to feeling low for both men and women – you should just pull your socks up and get on with it. Unfortunately, long-term low mood isn't likely to improve or disappear without treatment. If you have an ear infection you get antibiotics, if you have muscle ache you get a massage. Depression and low mood are no different – there are things you can do to feel better.

Work can be another reason to want to hide depression. According to mental health charity, MIND, one in six workers in the UK will be experiencing depression, anxiety or stress at any one time. While depression is classified as an illness, there's unfortunately still a stigma attached to admitting to employers and colleagues that you have a mental health issue. There's the terrifying fear that people might start treating you differently if you were to be signed off work because of your mood rather than, say, backache. Please be assured this kind of thinking is slowly, but surely changing. High-profile mental health campaigns such as 'Time to Change', England's biggest programme challenging mental health stigma and discrimination are doing wonders for educating people about the facts of feeling low. The truth is, you'd be hard pressed to find anyone who hasn't experienced some form of depression, either themselves or among their friends, family and colleagues.

What causes low mood?

The role that brain neurotransmitters play is still poorly understood, however most experts agree that depression cannot be diagnosed as simply the result of a chemical imbalance. Medical conditions have been known to trigger low mood. For example it can result from an underactive thyroid (hypothyroidism) or be a rare side effect of certain drugs such as beta blockers or some anti-epileptic drugs. (Please visit your GP if you believe this might be the case for you.) However, more commonly it is caused by a particular current stress, a culmination of stresses, a trauma or the impact of an early relationship (i.e. a destructive relationship with a parent or sibling).

Inevitably nature and nurture play their parts too. Research has found that in some cases genetics can influence our susceptibility to low mood, although not all depression is inherited. However, how you were raised will have shaped how confident you feel within yourself, how you deal with problems and how well you feel you can cope with emotional distress.

Our beliefs and impressions of the world and our view of ourselves and others are formed and developed in childhood. These beliefs tend to be centred round ideas of self-worth, achievement, acceptance and lovability. When you're a kid you accept what you are told (on the whole by your parents or those closest to you) as you often have no basis for comparison. Some of these childhood beliefs predispose us to low mood. For example, if you were given the impression that you were an ugly child or not clever enough, those thoughts may have been festering under the surface throughout your life leaving you feeling you don't quite measure up. While rationally you know that you're not ugly or stupid it's become a belief that you trust and on which other convictions are based.

What you're dealing with

There are a number of biological, social and psychological factors that can contribute to, or lead to, low mood, some of which may be affecting you. The list opposite gives examples.

Psychological

+ Current stressors e.g. the end of a relationship or difficulties at work
+ Feeling that you can't cope or don't know how to cope
+ Your temperament e.g. if you're very sensitive or prone to lashing out
+ Discovering upsetting things about yourself or not living up to your own expectations
+ Dwelling on troubling memories
+ Feeling hopeless or helpless
+ Interpreting events or situations in negative ways
+ Believing you are unlovable, worthless or inadequate

Biological

+ A genetic predisposition to depression
+ Being physically sensitive to changes in mood e.g. when stressed you'll feel achy or tense
+ A weak immune system
+ Physical health problems

Social

+ A poor social network
+ A lack of sense of belonging
+ Inadequate access to medical care
+ Unhelpful cultural traditions e.g. whether it's expected or acceptable to seek help or talk about emotional issues
+ Difficult social-economic conditions including uncertain future prospects, unemployment and poverty

Depression: An unfriendly illness

Amy was browsing magazines in the supermarket when she sensed someone looking at her. She slowly turned her head and caught a woman at the other end of the aisle staring. She realised it was Gabby – the woman she'd met at the gym a few months ago. They'd started hanging out together, meeting for coffees, going out for drinks and having a real laugh. Then suddenly Gabby had disappeared. Stopped answering her calls and even, as far as Amy could tell, stopped going to the gym. Amy had felt dumped. In fact, it was worse than being dumped because she could find no reason for it. It's not like they'd had a row or she'd met someone else!

Amy quickly picked up a magazine and started to leaf through it to buy herself some time.

'Er, hi,' a voice said tentatively at her shoulder, 'I'm Gabby.'

Amy nodded. 'I know. Hi! How are you?'

'Fine,' Gabby replied, smiling. 'I forgot you lived round here.'

Amy didn't know what to say, so kept quiet, smiling awkwardly.

'Shall we do coffee again soon? It's been too long,' Gabby asked.

'Definitely,' Amy replied.

'Great, see you soon,' Gabby said, before turning towards the tills as Amy waved her goodbye.

⋯ **Amy's negative thought spiral:** Gabby had introduced herself! Their acquaintance had been so meaningless and fleeting she probably didn't even remember Amy's name. Was she deliberately trying to make her feel small? And then she'd made the empty gesture of suggesting they go for a coffee even though she'd ignored all Amy's previous invitations!

What actually happened: Gabby didn't know whether Amy would remember her. Assuming she did would seem presumptuous seeing as Gabby had been the one who had gone AWOL. She had forgotten Amy lived round here and as Amy had been looking at her strangely, she'd just said the first thing that popped into her head to fill the silence. She knew she'd ignored Amy's last few texts, as she'd been so busy trying to sort out her dad's hospital visits. She would text her in the next few weeks to organise that coffee. She hoped Amy would say yes as she'd really enjoyed her company when they'd met previously.

The effects of low mood

Low mood shifts how we process information. It makes us think more negatively and tends to link to themes of loss, defeat, failure, worthlessness and unlovability. Our attention becomes biased and focuses on things we are unhappy with or that prove how badly we're doing. We'll overgeneralise specifics and use single incidents as evidence of everything being bad. We tend to spend too much time mulling over difficult or upsetting things that have happened.

This negative thinking affects not just how we view ourselves, but how we view the world generally. Our pasts become intermingled with our futures and the people we meet become actors in the grey-tinged world we now inhabit. We can shape and interpret their behaviour to suit our new way of thinking: 'Chris didn't smile at me in the lift. It must be because I messed up that meeting.'

Cognitive Behavioural Therapy (which shall henceforth be referred to as CBT) suggests that your mood will stay low because of these biases in the way you think. It's all about self-regard. When you're depressed you automatically devalue your achievements and compare yourself negatively to others. You stick a great big fat magnifying glass over what you consider your failures and view negative events as having lasting implications for self-worth while ignoring anything positive. Minor mistakes will prompt you to generalise about the bigger picture: 'I did that wrong because I do everything wrong.' If you get a new job it's only because the person you were up against didn't want it. That guy you fancy asks you out … but only because your far-more-attractive mate has a boyfriend. You'll also ruminate on things in the past and dwell on 'what ifs'. For example, you're made redundant, and are immediately offered another job. Instead of focusing on the positives ('this could be a new start; I was bored in my old job anyway') you'll wallow in self-doubt about why you were made redundant and how it's only a matter of time before it'll happen again. To top it all off, you are also far more likely to recall sad or bad memories. You'll then shape these to fit into your current mindset –

'this is just like when …' – and events that you thought you'd moved on from will suddenly seem like terrifying portents of horror to come.

You're like a particularly stubborn cult leader who is determined to believe that not only are you the centre of everything, but that everything is rubbish.

Your biases will include the following:
+ Underestimation of performance
+ Interpretation of specific failure as the story of your life ('everything happens to me')
+ Negative comparisons with others
+ Interpretations of others' comments as critical
+ An inability to see how your current 'deficiencies' can be remedied

Symptoms of low mood

On the following page we've listed some of the most common symptoms of low mood. You'll recognise many of them, but some might surprise you. For example, if you're an impatient person you may think snapping at people or being quite dismissive is just an aspect of your personality rather than a result of frustration with yourself for not living up to your own expectations. People often classify themselves as 'a pessimist' or 'a worrier' without looking for the reasons behind it.

Rather than being intimidating this list should actually be reassuring – how you're feeling and what you're experiencing is completely normal. Everyone goes through it and there are ways of tackling each and every one of these symptoms.

Common symptons of low mood

Moods/emotions

❏ Low-spirited
❏ Restless
❏ Numb or empty
❏ Unconnected to reality – feel like you're living in a dream
❏ Helpless
❏ Agitated and irritable
❏ Angry
❏ Defensive
❏ Frustrated
❏ Isolated and lonely
❏ Sad
❏ Bored
❏ Uninterested
❏ Impatient
❏ Frightened
❏ Anxious
❏ Guilty

Thoughts

- ❑ Worried and negative
- ❑ Self-focused (the whole world's out to get me/why does this always happen to me?)
- ❑ Blaming yourself (this is my fault/I always mess things up)
- ❑ Comparative (she wouldn't have messed this up)
- ❑ Fearing the worst
- ❑ Doubting your ability to cope
- ❑ Inability to concentrate
- ❑ Dislike yourself – low self-esteem
- ❑ Ruminating (dwelling on things and going over and over them)
- ❑ Bleak and despairing
- ❑ Mournful
- ❑ Suicidal

Physicality

- ❑ Tension in neck and shoulders – general aches and pains
- ❑ Muscular cramps and spasms
- ❑ Exhaustion
- ❑ Sleeping problems
- ❑ Sluggish
- ❑ Clumsy
- ❑ Fidgety

Behaviour

- ❑ Increased drinking/smoking/drug taking
- ❑ Over or under eating
- ❑ Procrastinating
- ❑ Avoidance
- ❑ Snapping at people
- ❑ Being distracted/not concentrating
- ❑ Stopping pleasurable activities/not looking after yourself
- ❑ Poor time management
- ❑ Difficulty making decisions
- ❑ Absenteeism/withdrawing (both professionally and socially)
- ❑ Forgetful (e.g. you forget your keys or to lock up/to call someone/you leave your wallet at home)
- ❑ Constantly seek reassurance

Next steps ...

We reckon that while all of this sounds familiar, it probably also sounds fairly terrifying. But please don't panic. Admitting you feel unhappy and want to do something about it is a huge part of feeling happier. Many people accept their low mood as an unchangeable part of their lives and resign themselves to just plodding through. That's nonsense – you can change how you feel.

This book is all about things you can do proactively in your day-to-day life to start thinking and behaving more positively. Adopt the techniques and strategies suggested into your routines and you'll soon have the tools to make yourself feel happier on your own terms.

Thoughts to take away

✓ Depression *is* curable

✓ You're not alone, no matter how lonely you feel

✓ You can change the negative bias in your head, so that you interpret things more positively

2

Cognitive Behavioural Therapy

Cognitive Behavioural Therapy (CBT) is one of the leading evidence-based treatments for low mood, providing strategies and techniques to make you feel happier. Here we explain how it works and why it will work for you.

CBT: Not as scary as it sounds …

Pioneered by Dr Aaron T. Beck in the 1960s, CBT is now recommended by the National Institute of Clinical Excellence (NICE) as a highly effective treatment for a wide variety of disorders from depression and anxiety, to insomnia and Obsessive Compulsive Disorder (OCD). It's focused on helping you understand the problems you're facing and will teach you strategies to manage the difficulties in your life. The term 'evidence-based' means it's been rigorously tested in trials and proven to improve low mood – basically there's no hocus-pocus involved. You'll see genuine results from the skills and techniques you'll be taught and these tools will last a lifetime. CBT is all about feeling better now, no matter what's happened to you in your past. Whatever you've been through these strategies will help. It's also time efficient: treatment doesn't last years and years. You can feel better in a matter of weeks if you really throw yourself into it.

Substantial research backs up how brilliant CBT is in alleviating and often curing the symptoms of depression.

It has been suggested that one of the main reasons CBT is so successful and people stick to it is because it's giving you control in a situation that otherwise feels very out of control. After all, you're the expert on yourself, right? CBT teaches you the skills to manage your problems so you can become your own therapist.

There's also a proven reduction in the risk of relapse compared to other types of treatment. So once you've had a go at it, it will keep working for you. The problem-solving strategies aren't only easy to adopt, but through repetition and practice will become second nature; life will just become more manageable as if by magic.

'There is nothing either good or bad, but thinking makes it so' (Shakespeare, Hamlet, Act 2, scene 2)

Shakespeare didn't just have a flair for iambic pentameter; he knew that it's not what happens to you, it's how you interpret it. Basically, when you're feeling low the way you think becomes all screwed up. How you interpret a situation will affect your physical response (tensing up, hunched shoulders, beating heart), your emotional response (low, anxious, angry, hard done by), and your behavioural response (snapping at people, hiding away).

Situation $\longrightarrow$ Negative interpretation of what's going on $\longrightarrow$

> Physical response
> Emotional response
> Behavioural response

The same event can have totally different meanings for different people. It can also have different meanings for the same person depending on when it happens.

When you're feeling low your negative emotional response to a situation will cause you to behave differently to how you would if you were feeling on top of the world. How you act can make how you feel and your situation a million times worse. (For example, your boss shouts at you so you shout back.) Low mood is a self-fulfilling prophecy. You think, 'everything is rubbish', and so act as if this is a foregone conclusion. Behaving badly or in ways that are out of character will only maintain the problem or make it worse.

Examples: Do any of these situations look familiar to you?

1 It's last thing on Friday afternoon, you receive an email asking you to head up a presentation to the company CEO being given first thing on Monday morning. You have to rush off a reply while managing a million other things before the office closes. You feel anxious and worried. Why did they leave it until now to tell you? How are you going to get it done? Why does this always happen to you? However, if you'd received the same email on Monday morning asking you to prepare for a presentation in a couple of days you'd feel calm and in control because you'd have time to plan.

2 Your friend calls you to let you know he's got his dream job. You are thrilled for him. You know how hard he's worked and how much this means to him. However, you can't help wondering why you haven't got your dream job yet, even though you've applied for a couple of positions that fit the bill. Perhaps you're just not good enough.

3 You and a friend have both been invited to a party on Saturday night. She can't wait. You, on the other hand, are dreading it. You've got a 'crisis meeting' scheduled with your sister during the day and she's in the middle of a messy divorce. She'll ⋯

⋯⋯ have spent all afternoon crying on your shoulder and you won't be in any kind of mood for a party. Your friend, however, is desperate to go and you feel obliged to accompany her.

Example: Jittery James

James sees his friend Ben standing at the bar of a pub in town. He waves and shouts out his name. Ben peers around, stares at James and then looks away and orders a drink.

Low mood thinking

'Wow, Ben just ignored me!' →

> **Body:** Tenses up
> **Feels:** Sad, worried, insecure or annoyed
> **Behaves:** Ignores him when he next sees him

Happier thinking

'He couldn't see me without his glasses.' →

> **Body:** Neutral
> **Feels:** Neutral, calm
> **Behaves:** Says hello at next opportunity

The way you think about a situation impacts on how you feel ⋯⋯

⋯⋮⋅ and as we've seen in this example it can drastically affect the outcome of an event. By thinking negatively, James might ignore his friend, potentially creating a problem where there wasn't one. A domino effect could then follow with Ben reciprocating and before you know it they're both giving each other the silent treatment with neither of them being sure why.

Even if Ben did deliberately ignore James, by approaching him they'd be able to deal with the problem rather than both feeling insecure and worried about it.

Starting to question your thoughts and their validity will help you formulate more credible alternatives to negative assumptions. You'll be able to test out different ways of interpreting your experiences, allowing yourself to respond to events in new and more helpful ways. So the next time you lose your house keys and get locked out you won't immediately think:

'These things always happen to me!' → depressed

'I'm going to be stuck out of here for hours and get a cold.' → anxiety

'Argh! I can't believe I did that again!' → anger

You might think instead:

'Thank goodness my neighbour has a spare set.' → happy

'Thank goodness I'm wearing a warm coat.' → happy

The big fat vicious circle

As we've seen low mood is the result of a big fat vicious circle. Distorted thinking leads to a generally negative outlook and then you feel anxious and guilty about how you're acting and feeling (unmotivated or impatient), blaming yourself ('I'm weak and useless') which only serves to exacerbate things. On top of this, you'll look for evidence to back up these feelings, telling yourself as in the example below: 'Hannah literally ran across the street to avoid me,' ignoring the fact she was merely avoiding a car. CBT breaks this pattern of behaviour

Behaviour
Blank Hannah when
next see her

**Event
interpretation**
Hannah ran over the
road to get away
from me

Physicality
Tense, heart beating,
palm sweating

Thoughts
'It's becasue she
thinks I'm boring
and useless'

Emotions
Feel anxious, sad
and defeated

to give you back control of your emotional state.

There are two routes to feeling better: changing how you think (cognition) and changing what you do (behaviour). CBT uses them both. The whole point of this form of therapy is to learn how to question these negative biases and distortions in the way you think (and therefore behave) and formulate realistic alternatives – alternatives that the deep, dark, sad part of your mind will accept.

Chain reactions

CBT starts by assessing your behaviour and encouraging you to do more of the things that make you feel good and happy. You're then in a better position to identify your distressing thoughts, step back from them, evaluate how reasonable they are, and acknowledge that they're mostly complete drivel. At the moment your mind is probably full of worst-case-scenario predictions so just by thinking more realistically and asking yourself 'is that true?' or 'is that likely?' you'll feel better. Your current mode of thinking is not working out for you – so ditch it.

If you want to make changes you really will have to try out the exercises. Experimenting with doing things differently is the only way to reinforce the ideas you'll read about. The emphasis is on solving problems and initiating behavioural change in your everyday life. There'll be some trial and error, but that's part of the process. If something doesn't work first time, you'll be in a better position to try again. If after a few goes you're still not sure, that's okay. Some things you'll really like and others you might not – just pick whatever works best for you.

Mind maps

The simple diagram below is called a mind map. Throughout the book they'll change shape slightly as we focus in particular on one of the four points: behaviour, emotions, physicality, thoughts but the basic principal – that all of those things are linked and rely on each other – is always the same:

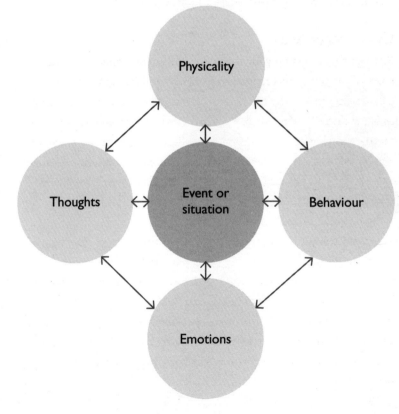

Your thoughts, behaviour and physicality act as intervention points. You can focus on any one of them and change them and this will have a positive influence on your mood. People stage interventions when someone is drinking or taking drugs: they all sit down in a circle and

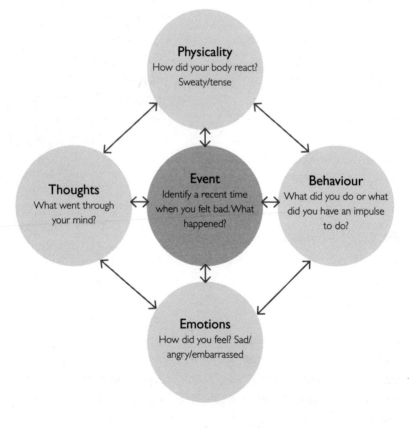

confront them with the realities of their life. Well, this is kind of the same – but you're confronting how you think, behave and feel and then intervening to change your negative tendencies to positive. Once you change one of them (say, your behaviour) the rest (with a bit of work) will follow.

You could just wait to feel happier, but who knows how long that will take? Paying attention to your own internal mind map will force you to reassess a situation and look at alternatives to your instinctive 'this is awful' interpretation. If what you are doing is part of the problem you can overhaul your day-to-day behaviour to start gaining a sense of achievement (even if it's just tiny things like taking out the bins) and also focus on doing stuff you enjoy to make yourself feel better. It's the same with thoughts and physical feelings. You can focus on them individually which will have a positive effect on your mood. Basically, the big fat circle will become less vicious, more chilled out and, most importantly, you'll feel happy.

⑤ Your own mind map

Think of a recent experience that left you feeling unhappy and have a go at filling in your own version of a mind map by going through each question in turn (starting in the middle).

This exercise enables you to start recognising your responses to an event – consciously separating your thoughts, behaviour and physical and emotional feelings so they're not all lumped together under the banner of 'Feeling Unhappy'. They're all separately contributing to how you feel, so writing this down and acknowledging it is the first step in understanding what's going on and taking action.

⑤ Thoughts aren't facts: Your new mantra in life

This sounds ridiculously simple and logical, but it's surprising how often we assume what we think is true without analysing the thought. When you think something, that's all it is: a thought, a hypothesis, an opinion. Unless you have incontrovertible proof to support your theory it remains just that – a theory. Don't give your negative thoughts any credit until you've taken time to assess them. If you reassess them we reckon you'll usually admit there's room for argument.

Example: Sarah's suspense – how should she think?

Sarah goes to the ladies. She hears two people walk in, talking and laughing. She recognises Claire's voice.

'Did you read Marie's email about her? Brutal!' Claire says.

'Yes I did,' the other girl answers, 'and then Marie freaked out because she thought she'd accidentally sent it straight to her!'

Sarah's initial thought (Theory A): 'They're talking about me.'
+ Her physical, emotional and behavioural responses go into panic overdrive: Sarah's heart is pumping, her palms are sweaty and she's trying to regulate her breathing.

Alternative (Theory B): 'I think they're talking about me.'
+ Sarah stops for a moment and then starts looking for proof. Has she had any run-ins with Marie lately? Has she done anything

---

⋯⋱ that would warrant an angry email? What's her relationship with Sarah and Claire like?

As long as Sarah recognises that it's a thought and not a fact she can take some time to work out how realistic it is that the two women are actually talking about her. This gives her time to develop the thoughts that will help her to come to a realistic conclusion.

Whenever you next catch yourself thinking something as if it's a fact, stop and analyse it. Remembering 'thoughts aren't facts' will stop you from jumping to conclusions and behaving rashly. It's a really simple exercise that we'll return to throughout the book.

Thoughts to take away

CBT will help you to:

✓ Overhaul what you're doing day-to-day to maximise a sense of achievement (even if it's just starting really small with 'do the washing') and also focus on doing more of the things you enjoy

✓ Rethink counter-productive beliefs and interpretations

✓ Adopt skills and strategies that will help change your situation so that you feel happier

3

Changing Your Behaviour

How you behave influences your thoughts, emotions and how you feel physically. You can become aware of negative behaviour patterns and change them, so that you can start doing more of the things that make you feel happy and fewer of the things that make you feel sad.

The dangers of inactivity

As illustrated in the previous chapter by the snazzy diagram, how you behave, think, and feel emotionally and physically are all interlinked. Think of the last thing you overheard someone say that was just so eye-wateringly stupid it made you despair of humankind. We'll bet that you either rolled your eyes or gave some form of withering look just from the recollection. See – your physical responses are linked to what you think and vice versa. Clever, eh?

When you feel low you often lose interest in what's going on around you and start putting things off. Even small things become difficult. Everyday tasks, like cleaning the dishes or the process involved in leaving the house (getting up, having a shower, getting dressed), become hugely arduous and exhausting. Just the prospect of starting something can send you into a panic. You'll stop doing stuff you actually enjoy because it all just seems so utterly pointless. You can end up withdrawing altogether, struggling to get out of bed in the morning and not wanting to leave the house. Things can begin to feel overwhelming. It's a slippery slope because by cutting out the stuff that gave you a sense of achievement and pleasure you're missing out on the things that naturally lifted your mood and made you feel happy.

When you start behaving insularly – through no fault of your own – life becomes repetitive and boring, filled only with work, TV, essential chores and sleep. You'll crave sleep – both physically (because you're tired), but also emotionally, as an escape route. You've limited contact (or cut it altogether) with friends and family, so you have no direct social support. And because you're doing less you have more time to think over everything that makes you unhappy. On top of all that, you start beating yourself up about the situation – about how you're letting everyone down, including yourself, by not doing all the stuff you're meant to be doing. Thoughts like 'I'm lazy and useless', will circle around your brain as you feel control over your life slipping through your fingers.

Wow, no wonder you're feeling miserable. But don't panic – there are simple steps and strategies to stop these destructive patterns of behaviour.

Remove pleasure from life: Life becomes emptier and even menial jobs become too much effort

Low mood: Fatigue, reduced motivation, unhappiness

Reducing activities: Stop socialising, don't answer the door or your phone, stop going to the gym

Reduced pleasure and sense of achievement: By only doing essential jobs you've lost any sense of purpose or fun

It's important to understand how the things you do in your life have an effect on you – both positive and negative. This way, you can start to recognise the activities that make you feel good and give them more prominence in your life.

Example: Anna's angst

Anna had been feeling rubbish for weeks. At first she thought her lethargy was the aftermath of a particularly severe cold she'd had, but her low mood wasn't shifting. She felt tired, ratty, defensive and, well, bored. Her previously 'amazing' job as a barista in a trendy coffee bar suddenly seemed trivial in the grand scheme of things. Who cares if the coffee is burned? Who cares where the sodding beans are from? She certainly didn't.

She started turning down invites from her friends. She knew they would realise she was feeling down if she was quiet and nag her about it. It wasn't as if she could tell them a concrete reason for her mood to keep them satisfied. Nothing majorly bad had happened for ages. She just felt sad. But how could she tell her friends that? So she said no to them. Secretly, she felt relieved when they accepted her excuses.

After a few weeks of no-shows Anna's friends started asking her what was wrong and if they'd done anything to upset her. Anna felt guilty so she started saying yes to the plans and then

⋯⋰ cancelling at the last minute. 'I'm having to work late/I got lost/I missed the train/I twisted my ankle on the way.'

She stayed at home, watching the telly and thinking – a lot. Mainly about what a bad friend she was for skipping out on her mates and what a bad person she was for not caring about her job.

Every morning she'd drag herself out of bed, go to work, slog through the day, go home and watch TV. And the longer it went on the worse she felt. The easiest thing to do was go to sleep because it didn't hurt so much when she was asleep.

⑨ Your own behavioural mind map

Now you've read about Anna's situation you can assess your own in a similar way. Think of a time recently when you didn't do something that you were either meant to do or that you usually would have wanted to do – be it missing a night out with friends, attending a gym class, seeing your gran or going to a club you normally love. Be really honest. It has to be something you know you could have gone to, but you didn't because you felt you couldn't face it.

How did missing the event make you feel – emotionally and physically? What went through your mind once you knew you were going to miss the event? What did you think when it was happening and you weren't there? Refer back to the questions in the mind map example on p38 if you need help getting started. Writing it all down

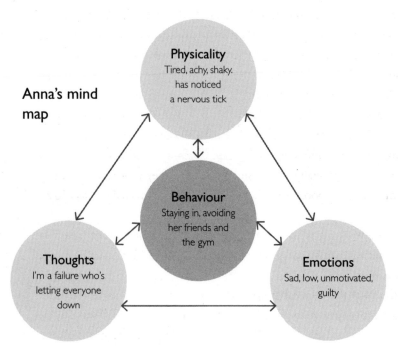

Anna's mind map

Physicality
Tired, achy, shaky.
has noticed
a nervous tick

Behaviour
Staying in, avoiding
her friends and
the gym

Thoughts
I'm a failure who's
letting everyone
down

Emotions
Sad, low, unmotivated,
guilty

will prove that there is a pattern to your behaviour and that your negative responses feed off each other. This pattern can be changed.

Behaving sadly

Anna's situation may not have rung true for you. Everyone's different and everyone behaves in different ways. Some people react in totally the opposite way to Anna when they're feeling low or depressed –

rather than becoming more introverted, they become the life and soul of the party (on the surface): a total extrovert. They accept every invitation no matter what. 'White water rafting in a swamp with someone I don't like? Yes please.' They don't care what it is as long as it'll keep them from spending too much time in their own head.

Depending on their social circles this can turn into a dependency on drink and drugs since alcohol and narcotics make people feel and appear more confident. They loosen the tongue and help you to feel you fit in, especially when you're unhappy. They give you a seemingly much needed boost for a few hours before the inevitable crash back to earth.

For someone who feels low, drink and drugs only exacerbate the problems and the self-guilt cycle. You'll behave out of character and you may have trouble remembering things you said or did – but you don't want to remember because it's frightening to acknowledge and admit that you were out of control. The only thing for it? Another drink, toke or line. The NHS estimates that approximately 4 per cent of women and 9 per cent of men in the UK show signs of alcohol dependency, while in the US, the National Institute of Alcohol Abuse and Alcoholism found 28.8 per cent of women and 43.1 per cent of men could be classed as binge drinkers (consuming four or five drinks within two hours at least once a year). Obviously, enjoying a drink doesn't make you an alcoholic, but if you are drinking more than usual it might be masking a deeper issue. If you come home every night (or morning) and feel just as low as you did the day before, no matter how good your night was, then you need to start dealing with the whys behind your behaviour. You won't be able to maintain that level of sociability and false camaraderie forever – which is when Anna's behaviour will start creeping into your own daily life. You'll stop going out and start hiding away. Going from one extreme to the other will be a huge shock to both you and your friends.

⑤ Curbing bad behaviour: the activity diary

Filling in the mind map has shown you how everything you do connects to how you feel and think. So it's logical (and true, we promise) that changing what you do can make you feel happier.

Say hello to your activity diary. We're going to be asking you to fill out a few diaries throughout the book to monitor what you're doing and to see the positive changes you're making. Please make sure you finish one diary before starting the next so the ones you're working on don't overlap. Keep a diary for one week and then review it at the end. It's really easy. Just write down what you do every day and rate your mood as you go, zero to ten. Zero is your worst mood and ten, your best. Also mark down activities you particularly enjoy as 'E' and things that give you a sense of achievment 'A'. Nothing is too small or insignificant. If you really enjoy eating breakfast put an E next to it. If you vaguely enjoy your tea break whack an 'E' next to that. If you feel a sense of achievement in getting out of bed and into the shower then write an 'A' next to that.

This diary isn't about how you think other people would rate your day – it's about how you rate your day. In the grand scheme of things getting out of bed and having a shower might not be considered a massive achievement, but on a day when you're feeling low it's a huge deal as your body and mind are screaming at you to do the opposite.

You shouldn't underestimate how strong you're being just getting through the day. It's time to start giving yourself some credit.

Filling out the diary will really force you to confront your daily activities, making you look at what you actually do and consider how it's making you feel. A lot of the time we go through life in a daze. Have you ever driven along a route you know like the back of your hand, arrived, and not even remembered getting there? It's because you're on autopilot, which can be dangerous because you're not aware of your surroundings, other people, and most importantly yourself. You might not even realise that you feel terrible driving to work. It's actually the lowest you feel all day because you're dreading arriving. Because you're on autopilot you haven't acknowledged those feelings and they just get lost into the big grey smudge of sadness. Filling in this table will force you to face your day head on.

This guideline table shows Monday filled out as an example, but you can structure it however suits you, perhaps by going through each day hour by hour.

How to fill in the table:
1 Write down what you do.
2 Give it a happiness rating on a scale of 0–10.
3 Take note of what you enjoyed and mark it with an 'E'.
4 Take note of when you felt any sense of achievement and mark it with an 'A'.

	Monday	Tuesday	Wednesday
MORNING	Get up **0**; have shower **3**; eat breakfast **4**; drive to work - **0**; arrive **0**; make cup of tea **4 E**; go through emails **5 A**; work **5**		
LUNCHTIME	Go to regular café **7**; order same sandwich I have every day **7**; have a cigarette **7 E**; go back to office **2**; look up celeb gossip online **6 E**; return friend's email **7 A**; make cup of tea **7**		
AFTERNOON	Work **5 A**; have tea break at 3p.m. **7**; finish work at 5p.m. **8**		
EVENING	Drive home **5**; microwave dinner **4**; eat and watch soap on TV **5**; look at what's happening on Facebook but don't post anything **4**		
NIGHT TIME	Go to bed at 10p.m. **3**; toss and turn **0**; finally get to sleep at 1a.m. **4**		

Fill in the activity diary as fully as possible for a week. When you've finished answer the following questions:

+ **Over the whole week what was your average mood rating?**
  (Add up all the numbers and then divide them by how many numbers there are.) This is your baseline, which you're going to improve on as you start to feel happier. You can check back in as you work through the book to see that your average mood rating is improving.

Thursday	Friday	Saturday	Sunday

◆ **When is your mood higher or lower?**
For most people their mood tends to be lowest in the morning. Just by getting out of bed your mood will already be on the way up (even though this is probably the worst bit of the day that needs the most self-motivation). Lying in bed with time to think makes it harder to get up which is why the 'snooze' button is so dangerous.

◆ **What are you doing when your mood is at its highest and its lowest?**

Mood fluctuates and it will no doubt vary throughout the day. Just because it's gone down that doesn't mean it will stay there. Putting things off is a classic way of sustaining a bad mood. Doing things as you become aware of them, even if it's something you dread, will make you feel better.

+ **How many 'E's and 'A's are there on the diary?**
Take note of all the things you marked. This will help you to identify the things you really enjoyed doing and that gave you a sense of achievement – your mood score was most likely higher when you were doing these things. If you have no 'E's and no 'A's then please reassess your chart. If there really was nothing that you enjoyed during an entire week then it's time to be pragmatic. Ask yourself this: what did you hate the least? What made you feel the least bad? Even if you didn't enjoy it as such, perhaps having a cup of tea or hot chocolate wasn't totally disagreeable. Put at 'E' next to those things. There's no shame in starting small.

+ **How many hours sleep did you get?**
Research recommends that adults need between six and eight hours' sleep a night to function well both physically and mentally. If you're regularly getting less than this or tossing and turning all night it can have a huge effect on your mood. In fact, sleep is such a big deal that we've written a whole book on it: *This Book Will Make You Sleep*. We also run through some strategies for improving your sleep in Chapter 5.

Assessing your activity diary will identify what actually makes you feel good and why. When you're feeling low all the time the peaks in your mood are often easy to miss. It's also important to note the activities that make you feel low and why so you can start doing fewer of them or balance them out more with things that you enjoy. Seeing your day broken down like this will enable you to start shifting the balance towards the positive.

Next steps …

Write 'BEHAVIOURS FAIL, NOT PEOPLE' in your notebook and read it whenever you feel worried or conflicted over something you've done. It will remind you that what you do doesn't have to represent who you are. What you did was bad, but that doesn't mean you are bad. Your behaviour does not define who you are – because you can change it.

Thoughts to take away

✓ What you do affects how you feel physically and emotionally and how you think, so behaving positively will have a positive knock-on effect

✓ Inactivity breeds negativity, whereas doing things you enjoy gives pleasure and a sense of achievement

✓ Recognising what makes you feel happy and what makes you feel sad is the first crucial step to changing negative patterns of behaviour

4

Making Time for Yourself

A key component of feeling happier is making the most of your time, concentrating on the things that make you feel good and cutting down or cutting out the things that make you feel low. Altering your routine is a simple, but effective way of feeling better.

Time to change

When you filled in the activity diary on pages 52–3 certain things you enjoy should have jumped out at you. As we mentioned it really doesn't matter how big or small those things were because we can build on all of it. (Apart from winning £25 million on the lottery; we can't recreate that kind of euphoria I'm afraid.) It's not just about recognising the things that made you feel happier, it's also important to take note of what made you feel bad. By acknowledging these low mood-provoking activities you're giving yourself three options:

1 Start trying to erase them from your day-to-day life.
2 Balance them out by doing more of the things you like.
3 Change how you approach them, altering how you feel about them.

Take the drive to work scenario from Chapter 3 as an example. If you scored it zero to three in your diary table, could being on autopilot be the problem? You're so physically and mentally used to the drive that you don't think about your surroundings, what you're doing; what you do think about is your dread of turning up to work and having to go through the motions for eight hours. The knot in your stomach is such a normal part of your commute that you've accepted it as a permanent fixture.

So what can you do about it?

Well, now you've recognised it you can choose to make changes. We've listed some ideas below:

+ Take a different route so you become more aware of your drive. You'll have to concentrate on what's around you rather than be locked in your own head.
+ Invest in some audio books so you can listen as you travel, taking your mind off work.
+ Turn your phone onto silent. Make the commute a work-free zone.
+ Introduce activities you do enjoy into the trip. If you love coffee, take a Thermos.
+ Become more aware of yourself in the car. Think about your breathing and talk yourself through what you're doing ('I'm changing gears now. I'm indicating to go left.'). It's a way of staying in the present and giving your mind a break. (We will explain this form of 'mindfulness' in Chapter 9.)
+ Open the window (whatever the weather), giving yourself a blast of fresh air.
+ Scrap the drive altogether if you can and find an alternative way to get to work – via bus, train, bike or good old-fashioned walking. Breaking up your behavioural routine will break up your head's routine too.

No matter what the situation there are lots of things you can do to change your behaviour and to help stop you ruminating on sadness. Pick out the activities from your diary that made you feel lowest and brainstorm alternative ways to approach them, as we've done with the drive to work. Subtle alterations to your routine will have a big positive effect.

Filling in the activity diary should also have raised a little internal red flag about punishing yourself for feeling sad. Now that you're aware of certain times when you're more likely to feel low you won't berate yourself so much. You might not even be aware you're doing it, but we bet you tell yourself off for feeling unmotivated. Now you know when you're more likely to feel at your worst you can cut yourself some slack at those times. Stop feeling bad about feeling sad.

A selfish salvation

We have 'be kind to others' drummed into us from childhood – we're told to share and give up our time to help those less fortunate, blah blah blah. Well, scrap it. Forget it. Right now what you actually need to be doing is looking after yourself, spending more time with you, yourself and [insert your own name here].

Being nice to yourself is a shortcut to feeling better. When you're low you often stop doing things for yourself. Ironically, it may feel like 'me time' is a luxury you can't afford, even when you're spending hours sitting on your sofa alone counting up all the ways you're letting everyone down. Sigh.

You might be one of those people whose role has always been 'The Listener', discussing other people's concerns and worries and feeling selfish even thinking about burdening others with your problems. You would hate for your friends to feel they couldn't talk to you, yet you're withholding hugely important things from them. You're not being fair to yourself at all.

You need to make positive time for yourself. 'Me breaks' will increase productivity and scheduling them into your daily routine will improve your mood. Fact. Giving yourself a break, whether it's from work or just your thoughts, is restorative and relaxing. Staring into space and wondering why you're so bloody sad is not relaxing. You also need to start focusing on doing the social things that you actually enjoy rather than those you feel obliged to do. Hanging out with other people on your own terms rather than under duress will mean you're much more likely to enjoy yourself!

⑤ Your 'me time' mind map

Fill in the mind map below with an activity from the diary that you enjoyed. Try to think of two activities – one you did on your own and one which involved other people. Assess how what you did made you feel emotionally and physically and also what your thoughts were at the time. We have filled out an example on page 62 to start you off.

A recent study found that doing at least one pleasurable activity every day will create a lasting improvement in your mood. Researchers discovered that the more time participants engaged in social activities (with friends or family), were physically active or were stretching their minds (by learning new things) the happier they reported being. By scheduling in at least one of these activities a day you'll not only feel good when you're actually doing them, but you'll feel better knowing you have something to look forward to the next day and the day after that. You're creating a pattern of positive behaviour. And it doesn't matter how small the activities are, even just scheduling in more tea breaks during work can make you feel more relaxed. The knowledge that you're being proactive about making changes will give you more control over your mood. The strategy below will help you to get more of these agreeable things into your diary.

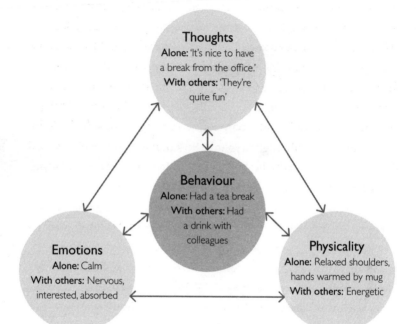

Thoughts
Alone: 'It's nice to have a break from the office.'
With others: 'They're quite fun'

Behaviour
Alone: Had a tea break
With others: Had a drink with colleagues

Emotions
Alone: Calm
With others: Nervous, interested, absorbed

Physicality
Alone: Relaxed shoulders, hands warmed by mug
With others: Energetic

⑤ Organised fun

While we're normally wary of compulsory good times (involving hideous team-building exercises with some prat brandishing a whistle), planning things you enjoy into your week is important. The next step is to create a new activity diary (make sure you've finished your first one before starting this one) in which you'll schedule at least one activity per day that makes you feel good – or if not good then at least okay. If you plan in specifics and commit to a day and time it's much more likely to happen rather than just thinking, 'Yeah, I'll do it sometime next week.' For example, instead of writing 'see friend', arrange it with him and write 'Monday 5.30p.m.: meet Mike at coffee shop'. Or if you enjoy jogging, schedule in a jog back from work on Monday and Friday. And on Tuesday make time to walk through that park you love at lunchtime, etc. Start by brainstorming a list of things you can do that you'd find fun, relaxing, exciting or interesting. Focus on activities that fully engage your attention, make you feel better and that you're good at, whether big or small. Here are some ideas to get you started:

+ If you enjoy drinking espressos from fancy-pants coffee shops then make time to visit one during your lunch break.
+ Social support is so important. Plan a meal with a friend and then book the table so you'll be more inclined not to cancel.
+ Make sure you have your favourite burrito for dinner and savour every mouthful.
+ Listen to a great album on the way to work.
+ Exercise. Nothing raises your energy faster and more effectively. (See Chapter 5.)
+ Look into volunteering for a charity – no one's going to turn down an extra pair of hands. Feeling helpful will hugely bolster your self-esteem.
+ Look at what you gave a higher mood rating in the activity diary,

try to recall some of the things you used to enjoy doing before you started feeling low or investigate ways of starting something you've always wanted to try be it painting, tennis or joining a book club.

Once you've settled on a couple of ideas from your brainstorm, write them into your activity diary and then stick to it. Plan one meaningful activity into each day of the next week, but be careful not to shoe-horn too much in so you can't keep up. We want this to be something that works for you rather than another thing to worry about. Make sure you give yourself enough time for everything as the extra pressure you put on yourself to complete each task might add to the problem. Remember a meaningful activity can be 'read a chapter of favourite novel'. If you find it hard to get started then categorise the activities into 'easy', 'medium' and 'hard', and work through the week adding in the 'easy' ones first.

As you go through the week, monitor your mood as you complete different tasks over the course of your day – just like you did for your first activity diary in the last chapter: 0–10 for mood (zero for saddest and 10 for happiest) and then 'E' for things you enjoyed and 'A' when you felt a sense of achievement. At the end of your week review your diary and assess how you feel about it.

✦ Do you feel better than you did during your first activity diary?
✦ What is your new average mood rating?
✦ Have you enjoyed more and felt that you achieved more?

If you have, congratulations! That is great news and shows you're making big steps towards feeling happier. If you haven't, don't worry. Just try to determine why it didn't work for you. Did you try to do too much? Did you try to do too many 'hard' things rather than mix in 'easy' and 'medium' activities? Try again next week and give yourself a break! If you felt even a little bit better than normal on one day of the week then that's progress.

Actually initiating change can be the hardest part, but once you have it's much easier to keep going. Picture yourself as a car (an Aston Martin Vanquish perhaps). You need a lot of power to get started, but then it gets easier and easier as you pick up speed and move through the gears.

Facing your fears

If the thought of altering your routine is frightening, note down the pros and cons of change. Write down why you want to do X and what's currently stopping you. For example, you might want to join a life-drawing class, but feel you don't have the time.

Pros
+ Meet new people
+ Learn a new skill
+ Reignite a passion for drawing

Cons
+ Each session takes two hours and I don't have time
+ It costs money and I'm trying to save
+ I'm scared I won't be any good

The pros massively outweigh the cons. Be aware of potential barriers your mind will try to throw in your way. Work around them. If you genuinely don't have two hours to spare then try to find a one-hour course that's closer to work or home. Also look into different courses to find one that costs less or negotiate with the organisers to see if you can get a discount if you pay upfront for several sessions. Your fear will subside once you've committed yourself to going and it will disappear altogether once you've beaten your demons and actually attended a class. It might turn into nervousness about how you're doing or whether you're fitting in or progressing, but that's totally normal. Everyone feels like that when they start something new. It's just getting over the original fear that stops you actually starting. Once you've done that the battle's won.

Thoughts to take away

✓ It can be good to be selfish. Stop doing things you don't enjoy or balance them out by doing more of the things you do

✓ Look for ways around obstacles. Making tiny changes will add up to a big difference

✓ Scheduling positive activities into your diary will make you feel more motivated and hopeful

5

Physical Education

Your mental health affects your physical health in a number of ways. Here we will examine how and why your body plays such a big role in determining how you feel emotionally, how you think and how you act, and offer strategies that will make you feel happier both in body and mind.

Physical education

There are strong links between how you feel emotionally and how you feel physically. When you're feeling low your body reacts to the signals pinging out from your brain causing your energy levels to drop. You can feel exhausted even if you haven't done much, or tired when you've had lots of sleep. Your concentration levels become non-existent, you'll fidget and become restless. Your memory will suffer and your sex-drive will fizzle to nothing. Depression can also affect your appetite, leaving you either totally uninterested in food or binge-eating. It can directly cause headaches, back pain and digestive problems. Because it's often easier to focus on the physical rather than the mental symptoms you're experiencing many people go to the doctor and explain all about their migraines and aches and pains without ever mentioning the deeper mental issues that are actually causing it all.

As if this was not enough, your sleeping patterns might become disrupted, leading to insomnia where your mind races into the small hours. Or you might wake in the night or early in the morning and find it impossible to get back to sleep. Alternatively you might feel you need to sleep all the time – your eyes snapping open to find your face stuck to your computer keyboard. Losing sleep will leave you mentally and physically drained.

Feeling like you've been hit by an angry freewheeling monster truck will inevitably have an impact on your emotions, your thoughts and your behaviour. It can seem like a never-ending cycle of hideousness – but don't worry, you can escape!

Comfort eating and fasting

Don't self-medicate with food. Both comfort eating and avoiding food will affect how you feel physically which, in turn, will have a negative effect on how you feel mentally. If you're eating less than normal your body will be trying to function on less fuel and energy so everything you do will feel harder. Imagine trying to drive a car by pedalling Fred Flintstone-style. That's what your poor underpowered body is going through. Plus, if your sugar levels are low you're more likely to experience headaches and tiredness, while if you're comfort eating you're going to be getting lots of sugar crashes which will make you feel sluggish, bloated or sick. A study by the *American Journal of Psychiatry* found that people who gorge on junk food have a much higher risk of suffering from low mood or depression.

Anorexia nervosa and bulimia nervosa

If you've been over- or under-eating for a long period, you're at risk of developing an eating disorder such as anorexia (severely restricting your food intake) or bulimia (extreme over-eating, followed by vomiting or fasting).

Eating disorders are all about control – you can find yourself controlling how much you eat and what you eat as a way of avoiding or deflecting attention from difficult issues or painful emotions. It never works though because while you're ⋯⋮⋅

⋯ controlling your food, you're losing control of how you feel emotionally and physically. You're not dealing with the real issue. If you're not feeling great mentally, punishing your body with bad food or no food is a form of self-harm and will only perpetuate your feelings of worthlessness.

If you think food is becoming an issue for you, it's essential you speak to your GP as they will be able to assess your individual case and recommend a specialist course of treatment.

A few diet dos

+ Eat whole grains or complex carbohydrates such as brown rice and beans. They increase the 'happy' chemical serotonin, which will boost your mood.
+ Munch B vitamins. Leafy green veg, beans, seeds and citrus fruits contain sources of folate, which helps to break down the amino acid homocysteine, which at high levels can work as a depressant.
+ Snack on yoghurt. Some studies have found that upping how much calcium you consume can up your mood.
+ Eat salmon. It contains omega-3 fatty acids and vitamin D (one of the few foods to do so) which can increase the levels of serotonin reaching your noggin.

✦ Nibble walnuts. These nuts contain omega-3 fatty acids and magnesium. Magnesium helps to stabilize mood by regulating blood sugar levels, it also helps you sleep, boosts your metabolism and enhances circulation.

Being positive with your diet is a failsafe way of feeling better both physically and mentally.

Let's get physical

People have known exercise is good for them since the first caveman felt a satisfying ache in his thighs after chasing a woolly mammoth. And it's true, exercising really will make you feel better. Nothing raises your energy levels faster and more effectively. It's been shown to be as helpful in reducing the symptoms of depression as antidepressants, individual psychotherapy, cognitive therapy and group psychology. Research has also found that an improvement in mood begins just ten minutes after you start exercising and this high gets better and better for up to twenty minutes. A study into exercise and depression in which participants walked daily for seven weeks found that their improved mood and vigour was still present five months later when they'd returned to their pre-trial routines.

What are endorphins?

Exercise makes you feel happier. Not only do you feel better about yourself for having taken positive action, but also because when you work out your body releases chemicals called endorphins. These are natural feel-good hormone-like substances produced in the brain and act as analgesics, meaning they diminish your perception of pain. When they're released by your neurotransmitters they go bouncing through your body giving you a feeling of euphoria. Exercise also releases adrenaline, serotonin and dopamine – these are all 'happy' chemicals that work together to make you feel great. Yes, you'll feel tired, but you'll also feel elated.

The positive effects of exercise

+ Increases endorphins
+ Increases well-being
+ Improves self-esteem
+ Gives a sense of achievement
+ Increases energy levels
+ Relieves stress and negative emotions
+ Improves motivation
+ Improves mental functioning
+ Improves sleep
+ Improves fitness and overall health
+ Provides opportunities to meet new people
+ Boosts morale

Ⓢ Actions really do speak louder than words

Remember, the point of exercise is not to become a potential Olympic candidate, it's to feel better about yourself physically and mentally. There's no sense in signing up for the next ultra-marathon and slogging for miles on a treadmill in a dingy gym for months on end if you haven't even been for a jog in years. You'll push yourself too far or you won't enjoy it. Saying, 'I'm going to go to the gym three times a week', when realistically it's never going to happen is a recipe for disaster. Instead, find something you enjoy doing that is achievable and realistic. Here are some suggestions for starting your 'New And Totally Unintimidating Exercise Regime' (that doesn't involve leg warmers unless you want it to):

+ Get off the bus a stop early. Exercising doesn't have to mean circuit training at a bootcamp. Doing anything more active is healthy. Why not just walk home rather than get the bus? Or walk up the stairs rather than take the lift?
+ Join a class. Most gyms have exercise classes that are open to non-members. Find one you like the sound of and go along to see what you think. Social support while exercising is very important – you're more likely to actually turn up if it means the chance for a chinwag and that you'll be letting someone else (other than yourself) down if you don't.
+ Try swimming for a low-impact cardiovascular workout.
+ After exercising have a sauna. A study by naturopathic physicians showed that sweating in a sauna can lower blood pressure, relieve muscle spasms, seasonal affective disorder and high stress levels.
+ Buy, borrow or hire a bike and cycle to work.
+ Go out dancing with your mates.
+ Make housework more energetic. Put on some music and dance about while hoovering, lunging to get into all the corners.
+ Do some gardening. It's very low-impact, but involves lots of bending, lunging, stretching and lifting.

✦ Try yoga or Pilates. Both these disciplines are hugely beneficial to body and mind.

Once you've decided what you want to try, adapt your activity diary and plan in some form of exercise at least three times a week for a 30-minute slot. Be specific, decide on a day and a time so you're more likely to do it and consider involving a friend so you're less likely to pull out at the last minute. Like you did previously when scheduling in positive activities, it could be helpful to list your chosen exercises into 'easy', 'medium' and 'hard' categories and then gradually work up to the ones you consider hard. Try to pick three different exercises to keep things interesting, whether it's walking, gardening or going to the gym.

Green exercise

A 2012 survey by the mental health charity, MIND, found that nine out of ten women aged over thirty, battle body confidence and low self-esteem when considering outdoor exercise. This is really sad because another survey by the same charity reported that 94 per cent of people tested said that 'green exercise' improved their mental health and sense of well-being. If you're insecure about jogging in public just walk around a park with some mates or your iPod, but don't hide away inside. Fresh air, nature and unfamiliar sights and sounds stimulate your body and mind.

Follow your new plan for one week, assess how it went and mark an 'E' or 'A' next to each exercise if you particularly enjoyed it or it gave you a sense of achievement.

Remember only do what you want to do, not what you think you should be doing. You're more likely to stick at it if it's not a drag. As you did in Chapter 4, think about what might stop you from exercising and brainstorm ways around the problem, e.g. Low motivation → go with a friend.

After the week is up, ask yourself these questions:

◆ How did you feel before doing the exercise – apprehensive/ nervous/excited/tired/bored?
◆ How did you feel during the exercise?
◆ How did you feel after doing the exercise?
◆ Look back at the list of benefits we ran through earlier in the chapter. Can you tick any of them off?

You'll probably notice that on the whole you didn't feel like exercising – in fact the prospect was really quite daunting – but once you started your session you actually quite enjoyed it, and afterwards you felt good and secretly proud of yourself. So on the days when you're feeling decidedly unmotivated remind yourself that this is no indication of how you'll feel after you've done it. Think how you'll feel if you skip it altogether: regretful and guilty. How many times have you been annoyed with yourself for not doing what you set out to do? Start small (by walking home, taking the stairs instead of the lift) and you'll be amazed at the sense of achievement and well-being you'll get. You'll

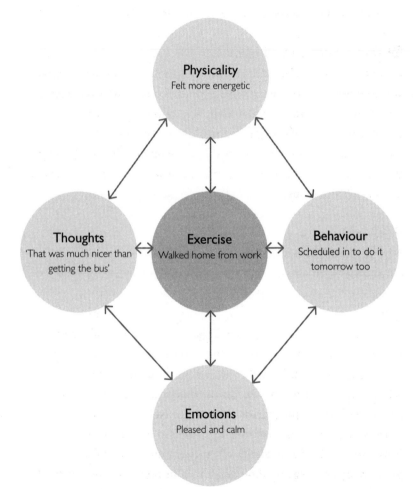

Physicality
Felt more energetic

Thoughts
'That was much nicer than getting the bus'

Exercise
Walked home from work

Behaviour
Scheduled in to do it tomorrow too

Emotions
Pleased and calm

not only get the physical buzz that comes from exercise, but also the mental buzz at being able to tick it off your to-do list.

⑤ Your exercise mind map

Fill in the physical mind map on the left, picking one of the exercises you completed in your activity diary. Really focus on how completing the exercise made you feel, physically and emotionally, what you thought as a result of doing it and what it prompted you to do. Did it make you think 'I could do that again?' (thoughts), while jogging up the stairs to your flat (behaviour), while you were feeling really proud of yourself (emotions)?

And relax ...

A huge part of physical well-being is relaxation. Giving your body a chance to rest and recuperate is an essential part of a healthy lifestyle. When you feel tense, uptight and anxious your body is under constant strain, so it follows that when your body feels calmer so will your mind. It is physically impossible to be stressed mentally when physically relaxed and vice versa. Relaxing has a positive impact on your thoughts, emotions and what you do. It can be as simple as scheduling in time to read the Sunday papers, to catch up on your favourite television programme or to have a bath.

However, as easy as it is to say 'I'm going to relax now', it's a lot harder to actually do. Especially when your mind is full of stress, guilt, worry and negative thoughts, and your body's aching and tired. Because of this you're being ordered (yes, ordered) to relax. We're advocating a course of compulsory relaxation, which ... er ... actually sounds a little stressful, but it's not. Schedule in some things that you find relaxing in your activity diary – we have suggested two tried and tested techniques to help you unwind: deep breathing and taking a bath.

⑤ Deep breathing

This deep-breathing exercise will only take a few minutes, yet, if you do it properly, will really help you to relax:

+ Place one hand on your chest and one hand on your abdomen.
+ Breathe slowly (preferably through your nose with your mouth shut).
+ As you inhale push your abdomen out against your hand – feel your abdomen expand and your hand rise.
+ Hold for two seconds.
+ Exhale slowly through your nose – feel your stomach deflate and your hand fall.
+ Smile as you exhale. Smiling actually makes you feel happier.
+ Think of something – a loved one, a sunny beach, a beautiful view.
+ Repeat four times.

That's pretty much as simple as it gets. It will lower your heart rate, calm your body down and, because you're concentrating on your breathing, your mind gets a well-deserved rest too.

⑤ A bath and beyond

Neil Morris, a psychologist at the University of Wolverhampton, studied eighty people who took a bath every day for a fortnight. He discovered that his participants' sense of general well-being improved dramatically. All the subjects noted how their pessimism about the future dropped, while feelings of hedonism increased. Morris put it down to a combination of quiet and comfort.

There is a sense of luxury about a bath – something a bit decadent. That you're giving yourself time to luxuriate in a tub full of warm – possibly scented – water feels almost extravagant. You're not performing the chore of washing so you can go to work, you're taking time out of the day to just chill out.

There are also proven physical benefits to bathing. A hot bath can stimulate circulation and cell movement, while adding Epsom salts can help ease arthritis, skin conditions, fluid retention and aches and pains. Epsom salts contain magnesium sulphate which helps keep the enzymes in your body doing what they're supposed to be doing and can strengthen the walls of your digestive tract. All this, just by relaxing in the tub.

Sleeping solutions

Sleeping badly is not only a common symptom of depression and low mood, but it can also be one of the causes. Not being able to sleep for any reason is frightening, exhausting and debilitating, but there are practical things you can do to limit the chances of a bad night no matter how riled up your mind is.

If you haven't been getting enough sleep plan to go to bed earlier for a couple of nights next week and schedule it into your diary. On those nights avoid surfing the web on your computer, iPad or tablet for at least two hours before you head to bed. Not only does logging on stimulate your mind, but studies have found the bright light emitted from such devices suppresses the normal night-time release of melatonin, the 'sleeping hormone'. The artificial light convinces your body that it's still daytime and so it doesn't prepare itself for sleep. If this happens night after night your body clock becomes confused as it stops expecting to drop off during those hours and your natural sleeping patterns are disrupted. Laying off all computerised gadgets for a period of time before bed allows your body to start its natural wind down routine and your mind to relax.

Also, remove any unnecessary noise from your bedroom (like loud ticking clocks), make sure where you're sleeping is as dark as possible (as light messes up melatonin production) and ensure your sleeping environment is actually conducive to sleep, i.e. don't try to drop off in an armchair in front of the telly or in a bed covered with clothes, books and bags.

Thoughts to take away

✓ Take care of your body, feeling better physically will make you feel better mentally

✓ Incorporate exercise into your life: start a new class or modify your habits to become more active

✓ Physical relaxation is an essential part of a healthy life – so schedule it in!

Emotion
Overload

How do our feelings affect our behaviour, our thoughts and our overall physical and mental health? Here, we explain what emotions are and how you can change your emotional default settings from 'always sad' to 'feeling happier'.

Why we're all so emotional

Emotions guide your beliefs and the meaning you give to things in your life. They colour your thoughts, affect what you do and how you feel physically. They are an essential part of who we are and how we survive. If we go back to the very essence of human behaviour (caveman-style), emotional distress guided people to seek help while signalling to others that something was wrong. Think of our ingrained fight or flight response. It's a primitive response to a perceived threat. As soon as we feel fear or a sudden shock, nerve cells fire off emergency signals releasing chemicals like adrenaline and cortisol into our bloodstream. Our pupils dilate to sharpen our sight, our heartbeat races to pump blood to our limbs and our awareness of pain diminishes. Our body and mind are primed to either fight or run away. If you have a fear of spiders and see one lolloping across the floor towards you your body has exactly the same reaction as it would if you were standing in the jungle eyeing up a lion. It's all triggered by your feelings – your body doesn't know that the spider isn't life-threatening, it's just doing what it's programmed to do. Also, it can't differentiate between a physical threat (e.g. facing someone waving a gun) or a psychological one (e.g. a job interview or going through a break-up).

And it's not just fear that provokes overt physical responses: when you're feeling sad, you cry; when you're embarrassed, you blush; and when you're angry, you scowl. And those are just the obvious ones. Your body changes in thousands of subtle ways to reflect how you feel.

Emotions are also intrinsically linked to behaviours and thoughts. For example, feeling low might prompt you to think 'I'm not good enough', just as thinking 'I'm not good enough' will make you feel

The bottling process

The phrase 'bottling it up' is often used to describe people who keep a tight rein on their emotions and internalise everything. The commonly accepted assumption is that people who bottle stuff up eventually explode – which is true. Humans aren't built to withstand that kind of internal emotional pressure. There will inevitably be physical and behavioural repercussions (e.g. suddenly screaming, 'SHUT UP OR I'LL GAFFER TAPE YOUR MOUTH!' at your colleague.) The emotional bit of our brain is like a saucepan filled with water. When things are good it sits there, sloshing about merrily. When we're stressed and dealing with more than normal it's as if more water has been poured in and the gas has been cranked up. It starts bubbling away. Eventually, if we don't manage to turn the heat down or get rid of some of the water, it'll boil over and even tiny things can tip it over the edge. Something always has to give. The more you ignore problems or shove them away to the back of your mind, the more likely it is that one day you'll explode. Facing your feelings and dealing with them will limit stress and anxiety.

low. Feelings can trigger certain thoughts and actions just as certain actions and thoughts can trigger feelings. It's all connected. Anger is often a response to feeling wronged, frustrated or guilty, while anxiety can make you timid or provoke a fight or flight response. Grief helps you get over a loss, while love brings you closer to others and changes your priorities. Happiness is attractive and inclusive – it makes you open, approachable and more willing to approach others yourself and it's closely connected to self-esteem and feeling confident with who you are.

Some emotions are more complicated – envy for example. Most behavioural responses to envy are negative. However, depending on the type of person you are, it also might motivate you to better yourself.

Feelings can act as an alert to help you understand what's going on in your life and what you need to pay attention to. They are the way humans process situations and experiences. As much as we'd like to feel happy all of the time, it's just not realistic – you were born with the ability to feel the full spectrum of emotions. Unfortunately feeling low often leads to experiencing more negative emotions – such as irritability, anger, despair, resentment, guilt and jealousy which can lead to feeling ashamed or frustrated. Often these emotions appear when you've been hiding how you feel and bottling things up. Acknowledging your feelings and confronting the reasons behind why you feel the way you do is an essential part of feeling happier.

⑤ The emotion picture

Use the chart on the right to track your negative emotions. Write down how you felt, what the trigger was and also what the consequences were. Recognising the link between how you're feeling, how you're thinking and what you're doing will give you more options to change negative patterns.

If you find it hard to identify the emotion, work through the other

Situation	Automatic thoughts	Emotional reaction	Physical reaction	Behavioural reaction
My boss undermined me in a meeting in front of everyone	'Everyone thinks I'm rubbish at my job.'	Embarrassment, anxiety, anger	Tensed up, blushed, sweaty palms	Stormed out of the meeting
My friend has planned her 30th birthday party the day before my wedding	'She's doing this to sabotage my wedding.'	Hurt, anger	Heart beating	Refuse to attend her birthday party
My friend only ever contacts me when he needs something	'He's using me for my contacts.'	Frustration, anger	Hunched shoulders, stomach ache	Send angry email refusing to help him any more

bits first, such as the physical feeling or what you thought. (We have included a couple of examples.)

Isolating the emotion and your responses to it will make you more aware of your default emotional settings and what causes them. Rather than just being swamped by an overwhelming feeling, it helps to understand the component parts. It will feel more manageable to see your emotional response broken down into thoughts, behaviour and how you feel physically – you'll get a perspective and clarity about not only yourself, but also the situation and how best to deal with it, and it will give you options so that you can make changes. In the first example, above, if you hadn't filled in the chart you may have only identified your emotional reactions as embarrassment and anger –

missing out anxiety. By isolating your immediate thought – 'Everyone thinks I'm rubbish at my job', you've identified that you're most concerned with what everyone thinks of your professional capabilities – not that they saw you belittled in a meeting. This is important because it means you can now focus on why you're anxious that people might be questioning your ability.

+ Do they have reason to question it?
+ Have you been letting things slip lately?
+ Is this a totally unfounded worry?

Rather than just accepting that you feel crushed, you can take action: – ask another colleague their opinion or ask for an extra pair of hands for a few weeks if you have too much on. Your proactive behaviour will then make you feel better emotionally and physically because you're not just wallowing, you're taking control.

Which column of the form did you find it easiest to fill out – your thoughts, emotions, physical responses or your behaviour? At the moment, for example, you might experience physical reactions very strongly and work from there. You might remember feeling really tense and your heart pounding, and then you recall that those physical symptoms were caused by the embarrassment you felt after your boss undermined you. How you feel physically is an easy clue to working out what else is going on. Alternatively, some people might pick up on their mood first. You remember feeling awful because you felt you were being undermined. Whatever you noticed initially is your starting point and you can start filling in the gaps from there.

Identifying the trigger – what actually started off this chain of responses – is really important. Negative reactions can snowball and it's easy to lose focus on what you're actually feeling anxious or low about. The more you get used to tracing things back to their source the more options you're giving yourself to make changes.

⑤ Manage your emotions

There are some simple and effective ways of managing your emotions. As you will have seen from the last strategy, how you feel is intrinsically linked to how you interpret specific events.

+ A pessimistic assessment of a situation can provoke damaging behaviour along with negative emotions and uncomfortable physical feelings. Remember that just because you feel a certain way about something doesn't mean everybody else does too; how you feel is not a reflection of how well you're doing. You may feel frustrated and undervalued at work while everyone else thinks you're doing brilliantly. When you feel low you'll have a very biased outlook so you'll look for proof to back up your 'I'm failing/I can't cope' view. Don't project your feelings onto others or use them as a measure of your progress or achievement as it's more than likely you're being very unfair on yourself.

+ While it's healthy and natural to have strong emotional responses to things that happen to us (as a way of processing what's going on so we can move forward), be aware of wallowing in corrosive emotions – believing that you're always getting a bad deal or that everything bad always happens to you. This will not only make you feel terrible, but also trapped in a bad place. Remember that negative behaviour will provoke negative outcomes so the way you're thinking about yourself will affect how others view you and what happens in your life. Thinking 'I'm rubbish' all the time can become a self-fulfilling prophecy as you avoid difficult tasks or procrastinate, meaning you don't complete things to the best of your ability, if at all.

✦ When you next find yourself generalising and undermining your own abilities, catch the thoughts, acknowledge them and then challenge them – are they true? Force yourself to counteract them by picking out a time when something great did happen to you or when you did really well. When you're next feeling terrible, ask yourself, 'Will this matter tomorrow, in a week, next year?' If not, who cares? Let it go.

✦ Be open and honest with yourself and with others about how you're feeling – it'll give you the means to move on. The act of vocalising how you feel can give you some much needed distance from the situation, helping you to process things in your head and people will be able to support you and help you through it.

✦ And finally, laugh. Snort with mirth at funny stuff and also, most importantly, at yourself. Researchers at Oxford University discovered laughing causes the body to release endorphins that act as natural painkillers. You really do feel better after a good belly-laugh. A group was split into two: one was made to watch fifteen minutes of so-called 'boring' programmes (such as golf tournaments – honestly); while the other watched fifteen minutes of comedy shows. Scientists found that the people who had recently howled with laughter were able to withstand 10 per cent more pain than they had done before watching the shows, while the other group were less able to bear pain. It's a fact – laughter really is the best medicine. Taking life and yourself too seriously is only going to make everything seem harder to bear. Finding the funny side will release tension physically and make you feel more able to cope.

Thoughts to take away

✓ Don't bottle up your emotions as you're likely to explode. Be open and honest with yourself and others about how you're feeling

✓ Thinking and acting positively will make you feel more positive

✓ You can't banish sadness from your life forever, but you can make sure you're not feeling it unnecessarily

7

Mind Games

We're going to introduce you to your Negative Automatic Thoughts (NATs). They're holding your positive thoughts to ransom and you're letting them get away with it. This chapter explains where they come from and how to combat them.

Where's your head at?

If a genie popped out of our slightly chipped teapot and offered us three no-strings-attached wishes, we know exactly what we'd ask for. After we'd complimented him on his harem pants and offered him a brew, we'd wish for buckets full of cash, a house overlooking George Clooney's in Lake Como and to be mind-readers. What could possibly be better or more important than knowing what everyone's thinking? Um, well, loads could, as a matter of fact. Have you stepped back and had a rummage through your own mind recently? We hate to break it to you, but there's some properly weird stuff going on in there.

We've discussed how the way you think directly affects how you feel both emotionally and physically and also how you behave. So chances are if you're feeling bad your thoughts won't be shouting, 'Hey, you're ace! You're the best thing since control pants!' They're far more likely to be heckling you, screaming, 'You're so lame! You can't do anything right. We're embarrassed to even be in your pathetic mind.' Have a look at our example mind map on the right showing the effect of your negative thoughts.

Thinking is automatic. A bit like breathing. You just think. That's it. Even when you're asleep your mind is churning away. What's happening now though is because you feel low your thoughts have become a massive downer. They're depressing. They're not pulling their weight. If you're constantly thinking dark thoughts you'll feel rubbish – it makes sense. But you're so used to focusing on all the bad stuff you don't even realise that's what you're doing. It's become a bad habit – like regularly forgetting to turn your hair straighteners off and then having a heart attack on the way to work. You don't even realise you're

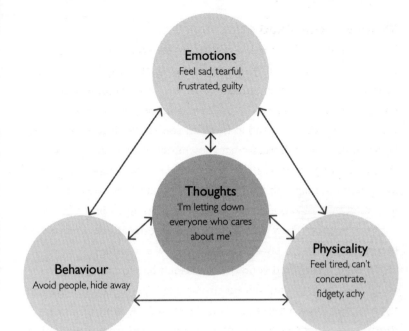

punishing yourself every single day because you've lost the ability to consciously register your thoughts.

Negative thought processing

When you go to bed you don't talk yourself through every little thing you do, such as: 'I'm going to pull back the covers, sit down, lift my left foot up and then my right foot before lying down.' You just get into bed while thinking about other things. This is down to 'thought processing' – how we manage all the thoughts in our head in an efficient way. Our brain chooses what's important to think about and what's not, siphoning off any information it considers inconsequential. This is integral to our being able to function properly, because if we had to really think about every tiny thing we did steam would come out of our ears.

This system works well … until your brain switches to negative autopilot and spotlights only that information which supports how bad you feel. Positive observations are ignored and you disregard important facts that would make you feel better and give you a more realistic and helpful view on what's happening. Your memory also plays a dastardly role, recalling only instances in your past that backs up your negative viewpoint. All of which inevitably maintains your low mood or makes you feel worse.

Negative processing becomes your default state of mind when you're low, but it goes into overdrive when you're feeling anxious and your fight or flight response kicks in. When your body feels under threat the rational part of your mind takes a back seat and the danger-detecting lobes take over. They are primed to hunt out any whiff of hazard in an attempt to keep you safe. This means not only are you focusing on the negatives as a matter of course, but you're more likely to assess neutral events as hostile, i.e. 'they're talking about me'.

When your head's working like this the only way to get a realistic view of what's going on is to actively seek out positive information to challenge your skewed way of thinking. You have to stand up to your negative automatic thoughts.

Negative Automatic Thoughts

+ NATs are the thoughts that whizz into your head without you even being aware of them. Things like 'Wow, she's much more successful than me,' or 'He hates me.' They are pessimistic appraisals and interpretations of things going on around you that you accept as facts.

+ NATs are habitual thoughts that you won't even really hear. They come and go as quickly as the last one-hit wonder. The trouble is they're usually vaguely plausible and so you take them as true despite the statement being unreasonable and unrealistic.

+ NATs make you feel terrible and get in the way of what's actually important.

+ NATs are contagious. One can quickly spiral into three, four or five.

Why NATs are the enemy and must be destroyed

Research shows that when you feel low your mind lays down the red carpet for NATs and welcomes them with open arms. CBT pioneer, Beck, found that NATs lead to misinterpretation of situations, selective attention to negative experiences and they'll also encourage your mind to block out any evidence that doesn't adhere to your gloomy view. In short: they're a nightmare and you have to get rid of them.

If you were aware of NATs each and every time they appeared and could stop and think about each thought objectively you'd no doubt discover you'd jumped to a conclusion that's total nonsense. However, most of the time you won't even be aware of them because they're so ingrained in your psyche. 'My boyfriend is getting bored with me'; 'I'm never going to get that promotion so I won't bother going for it';

'What's the point of going to the pub, no one will talk to me anyway'.

Even though you know that some (if not all) of your NATs are complete twaddle, they're still important. Why? Because they seemed completely reasonable to you at the time, which is confirmation that your mind is definitely processing information negatively. Allowing this to continue will only maintain your low mood or make it worse.

Channelling positive thoughts

When you feel low you have to proactively find good things to think about. Research shows that becoming more conscious of good events increases your happiness and decreases feelings of depression. Noticing and paying more attention to positives rather than negatives will tune your brain to do this more in the future – looking for good things will become a habit, correcting your negative bias and stopping you from dismissing favourable events or taking them for granted.

⑤ Think twice (or three times) about good things

In the next chapter we will analyse the twelve most common types of NATs and how they mess with your head. But for now shift your focus to take in the bigger picture. Next week think of three good things that happen to you every day. Yep, that's it. Just three good things – and then write them down in your notebook before you go to sleep. It could be that someone opened the door for you; or the bus driver saw you running and waited; or you dropped your phone, stopped and picked it up just as a bucket full of water fell off a ladder right where you would have been walking had you not stopped. Anything! Just think of them and write them down.

Example: Rach's date: NATs at work

Rach had been best friends with Tom for years. They'd always
been inseparable and people constantly asked her if they were
a couple. She'd always laughed it off before, but now started
wondering why they weren't. They found each other hilarious
(much to the annoyance of everyone else who didn't get their
'in' jokes) and they spent every spare minute together – but
nothing had ever happened between them. Rach gradually became
convinced that they were destined to be together forever, Tom
just hadn't realised it yet.

They'd always been very tactile, but now every touch or hug was
imbued with meaning. She made more effort with her appearance,
became unusually flirty and paid him lots of attention. Tom didn't
notice. After about three months of this, Rach started getting a
little despondent so was determined to either say something or
just lunge at him. She'd even worked out the pros and cons of a
just grabbing him for a kiss:

Pros: He might kiss me back in which case this will be the start of
a life-changing relationship.

Cons: He might reject me in which case I'll just blame the drink and
laugh the whole thing off. Ha ha ha.

⋯⋰ The next time everyone went out, Rach was ready. She'd spent days psyching herself up for this moment. She was preened to within an inch of her life and felt gorgeous, funny, clever and sexy. Tom then turned up and introduced everyone to his new girlfriend, Alex.

Alex was gorgeous, funny, clever and sexy.

Alex was two years younger than Rach.

Alex had an amazing job where she earned loads of cash.

Alex complimented Rach's new dress.

Alex was Tom's new Rach.

Rach made her excuses that night and left early. She didn't feel okay for the next few months. Her thoughts during that time could be summed up below:

+ I'm the biggest prat of all time
+ Everyone's either laughing at me or pitying me
+ How could I ever think someone that amazing would fancy me?
+ I've just lost my best mate because I'm such a berk
+ I'm never going to find someone as perfect for me as Tom
+ I despise everyone who has a happy relationship

Over the next week, reflect on why they happened. This is the most important bit. It's up to you to determine why things happen and to find the positives in them. For example, you might decide the bus driver waited for you because you smiled at him or just because he's a nice guy. Or you might think you didn't get splashed by the bucket of water because it's your lucky day. These reasons will make you see the world – and by reflection yourself – in a more positive light.

Feeling grateful

Properly paying attention to happier things (by writing them down) is a simple way to lift your mood and allow positive thoughts and emotions in. People who appreciate what they have see reasons to be grateful for what happens to them, look on the bright side and tend to be happier, healthier and more fulfilled. Studies show that gratitude can increase levels of well-being amongst those who cultivate it. Feeling grateful yourself and expressing appreciation to others will make you feel more energetic, optimistic and empathetic. People who undertook this 'Think Twice' strategy for just one week reported feeling happier up to six months later so there's no reason to stop after one week if it's working for you. Build it into your daily routine and you'll quickly notice a lift in your mood.

⑤ Your positive mind map

Pick one of the events that you noted down in the 'Think twice' strategy and fill out a mind map focusing on how you felt when it happened both physically and emotionally, your thoughts about it and what it made you do. We have included an example below.

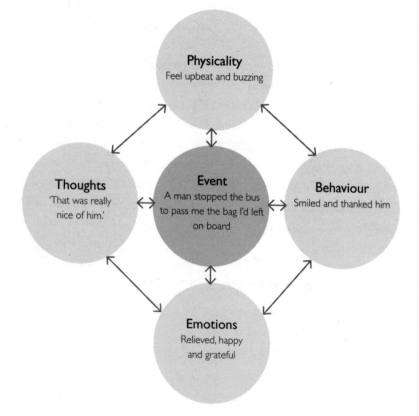

Physicality
Feel upbeat and buzzing

Thoughts
'That was really nice of him.'

Event
A man stopped the bus to pass me the bag I'd left on board

Behaviour
Smiled and thanked him

Emotions
Relieved, happy and grateful

Filling this out should prove to you that thinking positively is contagious – you'll feel better, behave better and feel physically better.

Thought crimes

Now you understand what NATs are it's important to learn where they come from so you can cut them off at the source. When you're stressed or tired, your insecurities increase, which is life's hilarious way of testing you. Feel hopeless? Need some reassurance? 'Well,' say your thoughts, 'that's not really surprising because you are hopeless. Everyone else is a million times better than you.' With the onslaught of social media there are now additional opportunities for paranoid comparison and second-guessing. Via this non-verbal route of 'speaking' to people you don't even have the luxury of the usual tonal or visual clues from your 'conversation'. Why didn't she put a kiss at the end of that email like she normally does? Did he write 'LOL' ironically? Is she joking when she says 'shut up' or is she genuinely annoyed? Every click of a button offers a glorious opportunity for self-doubt – but you can combat this.

Three biggest thought crimes against happiness

1 Comparing yourself to others.
2 Setting yourself up for a fall.
3 Dwelling on all the bad stuff.

Thought crime 1: Comparing yourself to others

Comparing yourself to someone else is natural. Everyone does this – it's part of human nature: survival of the fittest. However, when you're feeling sad, your comparisons become really damaging and totally unfair as you only compare yourself to those you perceive to be better than you (upwards comparisons) – ignoring anyone who is worse off (downward comparisons). You'll deliberately pick all your worst bits – the parts of yourself that you've never been confident about – and compare them to the best bits of your friends, colleagues or total strangers. You'll think, 'Alice has achieved so much more than me and we're the same age,' rather than, 'Alice has achieved so much because her tyrannical father punishes her if she doesn't.' Or, 'Stacy has such a perfect husband, while I don't even have a boyfriend,' rather than, 'It's lucky Stacy has such a great husband who puts up with living with his mother-in-law.' You might also compare yourself to celebrities, 'I'll never look like Scarlett Johansson.' Of course you won't! Scarlett Johansson doesn't even look like Scarlett Johansson if you take away the personal trainers, chefs, make-up artists and stylists. (No offence, Scarlett.)

Any information that serves to put you in a better position – or to see things more equally – gets ignored. If it doesn't fit in with your negative view of yourself you scrap it.

⑤ Combatting comparisons

Next time you find yourself comparing yourself to someone make sure it's a fair comparison – both to you and to them. And if they are really doing better than you, use it as inspiration: 'If Alice can do it and we're not that different, maybe I can too.' Or better yet, don't compare yourself at all. Instead concentrate on things that are going well in your life, set your own goals and focus on building up your confidence instead of pointlessly using all your energy to find areas where you believe you fall short.

Thought crime 2: Setting yourself up for a fall

If you feel low you might see things going wrong (often stuff that's completely out of your control) as a sign of your personal inadequacy. You'll set yourself completely unrealistic standards, promising that if you can achieve them it'll make you feel better. You inevitably don't – because no one could or it's totally out of your hands. 'I'll have a new job by this time next month'; 'I'll be pregnant by this time next year'; 'I'll get a per cent pay rise at my next assessment meeting.' When you don't meet these goals you'll feel intensely self-critical: 'Other people have done it – why couldn't I?' 'I'm always messing stuff up.' You'll also constantly move the goalposts so even if you do succeed in what you set out to do it no longer matters because your personal qualifications for 'success' have changed.

No one is perfect. No one. Not even the ridiculously attractive man next door with the high-flying job in advertising (he's actually just taken out another loan which he can't afford to pay off). You will always fail if you're trying to match up to an impossible ideal. It's like self-harm – you're 99 per cent sure you won't achieve it and almost look forward to hating yourself for it.

It's time to stop.

Don't aim for the unobtainable and stop punishing yourself for failing to meet unrealistic goals. If we followed you around all day whispering the horrible things you're saying to yourself, you'd think we were hideous bullies and yet you're constantly bullying yourself and you don't even realise it. You might tell yourself it's motivating you to work harder and get more done, but in reality it's leaving you feeling demotivated and a failure.

Criticism can be healthy if it's constructive and impartial, but self-criticism rarely is. You've programmed your thoughts to always be negative and so while a personal trainer might bellow, 'You're slacking, come on!' he'd usually qualify it with 'That's much better!' Most coaches and teachers know that constructive criticism has to be balanced with praise if you want to successfully motivate anyone. Only telling someone their bad points will destroy their motivation and ultimately make them want to give up.

⑤ Give yourself some friendly advice

Next time you feel you're struggling, assess the issue as you would for a friend. Basically, try being compassionate rather than critical and look for your strengths as well as areas where you can improve. If your friend came to you for help, your gut-instinct would be to be reassuring and encouraging, so channel some of that good stuff inwards. Ask yourself 'What would X say?' if you ran it past them. (And make sure X is a reasonable and fair person, not your nemesis.) Try putting the advice you think they'd give you into action. Stepping back from the issue might make you realise you've blown some things out of proportion, it's not actually that big a deal or you need to come at it from a different angle. Looking at it this way you'll be much more likely to make positive progress with whatever's troubling you.

Thought crime 3: Dwelling on all the bad stuff

When you feel depressed you underestimate your ability to cope so when a setback leads to a NAT it feels as though you'll never get over it. It's like seeing the world through fogged-up glasses. Everything's darker and sadder. Everything has a negative bias and you're even more likely to recall negative memories.

And it's not just the original NAT that's making you feel bad – that one soon spirals into more:

'Wow, that was rubbish' ➜ 'Nothing goes right for me any more' ➜ 'Life is so unfair' ➜ 'I should just give up'

Or

'I'm wasting my time' ➜ 'Nothing will ever make me feel better' ➜ 'No one even cares what I do' ➜ 'I should just give up'

This tendency to make sweeping generalisations when we feel terrible is really common. Something that happened to you personally becomes a representation of worldwide unfairness. You'll shift from the reality of what's going on around you to what's going on in your head. Yet, despite thinking things over for days, weeks, months, you're not actually progressing. You're not actually doing anything to solve the problem, you're just dwelling on it.

⑤ The dwelling test

Whenever you dwell on a negative experience you physically as well as mentally relive it. Take this dwelling test by focusing on each scenario in turn.

+ Think about the best meal you ever had. Picture the food on your plate. Admire it. Then imagine it on your fork going into your mouth. Remember everything about the taste on your tongue. Is your mouth watering?
+ Now think about someone you really fancy. Fantasise about them in a compromising situation that turns you on. If you're really concentrating on the thought you should get a thrill through your body. A tingle in your fingers. Butterflies in your stomach. Your eyes might even dilate.
+ Remember the worst, most embarrassing thing you've ever done while drunk. Relive the moment in all its grim horror. Are you blushing or cringing?
+ Recall the scariest horror film you've ever seen. Put yourself back in the moment and imagine it's happening to you. Right now. Your heart rate should increase, you might feel a prickle of sweat. An uncomfortable tightening sensation in your chest.

Thoughts, imagination and memories really do stimulate how we feel emotionally and physically, so the next time you find yourself dwelling on something use your feelings as a guide to learning when to stop. Ask yourself 'How do I feel?' If the answer is 'bad' then stop and shift your attention to something else. Consciously choose to think about and do other things. Say to yourself, 'This isn't getting me anywhere' (which is true otherwise you wouldn't be ruminating) and focus your attention elsewhere, whether it's making a cup of tea, phoning a friend or going for a run. Trust your feelings – why continue to make yourself feel bad?

Write down some encouraging phrases on Post-it notes and secrete them away in places you can find when you're feeling down. For example, if you have a nightmare boss write 'It's their problem' on a note and whenever they're being particularly horrible, just sneak a peek at it and remind yourself that, damn right it's their problem. Thoughts can't change the future or unpick the past so ruminating or dwelling on negatives is a waste of time. Instead use what you know now to make a positive plan for what to do next.

Thoughts to take away

✓ Cultivate optimism – look for the good things

✓ Thoughts are not facts! Recognise your NATs as they whizz through your head

✓ Be fair – if you're going to focus on what's not going well, then pay the same attention to what is going well. Be your own cheerleader!

8

Who Do You Think You Are?

The twelve most common and most dangerous NATs are introduced, assessed and, most importantly, neutralised here. Understanding what they are will give you the means to destroy them whenever they next scuttle through your head.

I think therefore I am

Now you're aware of NATs and how dangerous they are, you'll be more suspicious of them when they start stampeding through your head like a herd of bleating goats. There are twelve different species of NAT and we've described them all here. Unfortunately, when you're feeling unhappy it's pretty much guaranteed that all of these will make an appearance sooner or later. Equip yourself with our golden rules to fend them off.

Monochrome

Everything is clear-cut, black and white. If your performance falls short of perfect, you're a total failure. You set yourself ridiculous goals that are almost impossible to achieve just so you can punish yourself. If you somehow magically do reach your goal you'll find something, anything, to chastise yourself about. That £3,000 pay rise? It should have been £5,000. That four-minute mile? Should have been three.

Golden rule: Allow yourself to see the middle ground between good and bad or perfect and failure. Set yourself a realistic goal and promise yourself that if you achieve it, you'll give yourself a pat on the back. Then do it.

Overgeneralisation

You see a single negative event as a never-ending pattern. Didn't get that promotion? That's because you never get promoted. That man you liked who fancied your friend? That's because men always fancy your friend. Your thought patterns are characterised by the words 'never' and 'always'.

Golden rule: Change 'never' and 'always' to 'not this time' or 'sometimes'.

Nit picking

You pick out a single negative detail and dwell on it exclusively, thus losing any perspective on the event as a whole. It's like finding a tiny hairline crack on your favourite mug and suddenly hating the entire kitchen. You gave an amazing presentation at work, but stumbled over the word 'antidisestablishmentarianism' about three minutes in. Who cares, right? It even got a few laughs. Well, you care. You shouldn't have stumbled. What kind of idiot stumbles on that word? And you know they were really laughing at you, not with you.

Golden rule: You need to put things in perspective. If 99 per cent of something was great and 1 per cent bad then give 99 per cent of your attention to the great things and 1 per cent to the rest.

Positive shmositive

You reject a positive experience by insisting it 'doesn't count' for whatever reason, just so you can maintain your negative beliefs. After moaning about your boss for weeks, saying she doesn't appreciate you and takes you for granted, she sends a round-robin email to the entire company thanking you for all your hard work. Great, right? Well, no. She must have heard you'd been whining about her and this is her subtle revenge to let you know she's onto you.

Golden rule: Find a balance and be fair to yourself. Accept that good things do happen and when they're the result of your actions give yourself some credit. Rewarding yourself for your achievements is motivational and will drive you to succeed.

Telepathic trickery

No, you can't read minds, sorry. A raised eyebrow and squinty eye doesn't necessarily mean someone is plotting your immediate downfall. You're second-guessing something that hasn't happened and your analysis will be coloured by however you're feeling at the time. If you were feeling on top of the world and you caught your friend smirking at you, you'd probably think, 'Ha! I must be grinning like a lunatic!' But if you caught her smirking while feeling very insecure, you'd think, 'She reckons I've just made a fool of myself.'

Golden rule: No one can read minds, so don't second guess what others are thinking, especially when you're feeling down. Better yet, just ask what the person's thinking if you want to know that badly.

The fortune teller's error

You anticipate that things will turn out badly, and behave as though this is an established fact. This might make people think you're endearingly self-deprecating for a couple of days, but after a while it just seems self-indulgent. Assuming the worst will happen becomes a self-fulfilling prophecy as you behave in negative ways. Be careful: if you keep saying, 'Nah, I'm not good enough for that', other people will start believing it too.

Golden rule: Scrap the self-bullying because you can't win. If you do well, you disregard it, whereas if you do badly, you won't feel better by being proved right. Behaving positively will encourage positive results. Switch negative predictions to encouragement and self-belief.

The reverse binoculars

You exaggerate the importance of your mistakes while playing down the importance of your accomplishments. 'Oh, winning that award? Whatever. I just properly messed up that last assignment.' It's a sign of maturity to be able to accept a compliment. There's being modest and then there's being a bit rude. Remember that by belittling your achievements you're indirectly belittling other people's achievements too. If you're rubbish even though you won that award, what does that say about the people who didn't win?

Golden rule: Acknowledge that you've got to where you are today because of your accomplishments, not your mistakes.

Catastrophising

You attribute extreme and horrible consequences to the outcomes of events, making them seem unmanageable or interminable. 'If I see her at that party, I'll end up crying and ruining it for everyone. Best I just don't go.' The world isn't going to self-combust if you mess up occasionally.

Golden rule: Scrap the 'what ifs' altogether. You're worrying about something that hasn't happened yet and that probably never will. Ask yourself, 'What's realistically the worst that might happen?' and then, 'If the worst does happen, can I cope with it?' Have faith in what you can deal with and manage.

I'm sad therefore everything is sad

You assume that your negative emotions reflect the way things really are: 'I feel it, therefore it must be true.' You create a bad day when there's no need. You'll pass on your bad mood like a particularly virulent strain of flu. 'Isn't it a hideous day?' 'Wasn't that meeting mind-numbing?'

Golden rule: Just because you feel rubbish it doesn't mean rubbish things are going to happen. Don't use your feelings as a guide for how things will turn out, instead use the theory of 'opposite action': doing the things you least want to. Depression wants you to stay in and feel useless, therefore by disobeying depression and doing things that seem frightening or too much effort – seeing your friends, going to work – you'll feel better on so many levels.

Shoulda, woulda, coulda

You try to motivate yourself with shoulds and shouldn'ts, as if you need to be whipped or punished. 'I should have smiled when I saw the boss. Now he'll think I'm a miserable cow, or 'I shouldn't have smiled when I saw the boss. Now he'll think I'm a gormless idiot.'

Golden rule: Change the word 'should', to the far more life-affirming 'would/will' or 'could/can' so the thought becomes 'It would have been good to smile/not smile at the boss. I will do it/won't do it next time.' Or 'I could have smiled at the boss. I can do it next time.'

Why always me?

You believe negative events result from your own character flaws and you take responsibility for things that have nothing to do with you. Basically everything is about you. You are the centre of the sad universe, but because you're being pessimistic and self-defamatory you don't recognise it as egotistical or self-involved. Self-obsession can be as much part of the 'I'm worthless' mode of thinking as the 'I'm fabulous' thoughts. For example, if something breaks you'll think, 'I'm so clumsy', rather than, 'an accident, what a shame'. Or if someone looks miserable you'll think, 'she always scowls at me,' rather than, 'she always scowls.'.

Golden rule: Remember: it's not all about you. Next time you think something negative, try not to personalise it – take out the 'you' aspect and look at it in a wider context.

Savour failure

Okay, so something dreadful has happened, but you replay it over and over again in your mind. You're obsessed with it. You get a weird sense of satisfaction in making yourself relive the pain of the event hourly. You don't believe you deserve to feel okay. You can't see how you will ever feel okay again.

Golden rule: Be proactive about moving on. So, it was bad, but was it really the end of the world? And if yes, it was indeed the end of the world, then start trying to work out how you can get over it or learn from it. You can choose to either ruminate or reflect. Rumination means dwelling on something you cannot change, while reflection means using what you now know to move on.

Re-assessing her NATs from an outsider's perspective encouraged Rach to see her position differently. We asked her to fill out a mind map based upon this new perspective.

Rach's Date continued ...

After feeling rubbish for months, Rach finally spoke to a professional who managed to stop her cycle of self-recrimination and encouraged her to reassess her NATs. Rach's shock at what had happened had completely altered her outlook on life. She had to get the old Rach back. She wrote down the thoughts that summarised how she felt and answered them as if she were giving a friend advice using the golden rules for guidance. This is what she came up with:

✦ 'I'm so embarrassed I can't face anyone ever again.'
   Catastrophising
   You actually didn't do anything that embarrassing at all. It could have been a billion times worse. All you did, in the grand scheme of things, is fancy your friend. ⋯⋮⋅

◆ 'Everyone's either laughing at me or pitying me.'
Telepathic trickery
Stop trying to read people's minds. Just because you haven't
stopped thinking about it, doesn't mean everyone else hasn't.
You're not the first person to fancy someone who doesn't fancy
you back. Everyone's been there and your pride will get over it
eventually. At least you had the guts to give it a go.

◆ 'Every time I think about what's happened I burn with shame.'
Savour failure
Only because you can't believe you got it so wrong. On
the positive side at least now you know and aren't always
wondering 'what if?' How many times has someone liked you,
and you didn't reciprocate the feeling? You don't think any less
of the person so why should Tom think any less of you – I bet
he's flattered!

◆ 'I'm never going to find someone as perfect for me as Tom.'
Fortune teller's error
You can't predict the future and there's no reason to think you
won't find someone great. Tom never was perfect for you or
he'd be with you. Harsh, but true.

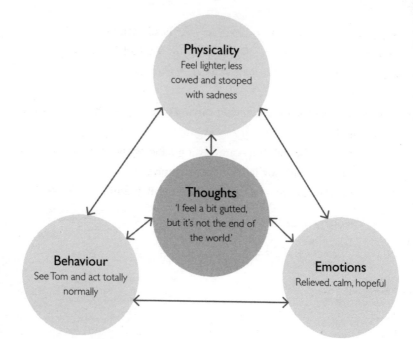

⑤ Your NAT mind map

Now it's your turn. Choose the last negative thought you had that really affected you and write it into the mind map. Look at it. How did it make you feel emotionally? (Sad, angry, scared, embarrassed?) How did that make you feel physically? (Did you clench your fists, get sweaty, feel an increase in your heart rate, get shaky hands, feel sick or tired?) And what did it make you do? (Go quiet, ignore questions you knew the answer to, storm off, pick an argument, get defensive?)

Just the act of writing it down and acknowledging this negative automatic thought will make you more aware of how they work.

Rather than allowing it to run riot in your head, noticing it will allow you to identify what is actually making you feel bad. You'll then have three choices:

1 Acknowledge the thought, accept it and carry on feeling bad or start feeling worse.
2 Acknowledge the thought – and let it go. Recognise it for what it was, but then don't pay it any more attention.
3 Acknowledge the thought and challenge it. Remember thoughts aren't facts!

We're strong advocates of the second two options.

Mindfulness

In the choices listed above, option 2 may have struck you as a bit odd. How can you listen to your negative thoughts, but then just let them go? It's a good question, but it is possible. While we fully believe you need to fundamentally change your way of thinking so you don't experience NATs at all any more or at least not as much (see Chapter 9), it can be a difficult process. So while you're working on that there is something you can do to alleviate the pain NATs cause.

In Chapter 5 we mentioned becoming more aware of yourself during your commute to work by taking note of your body and what's around you – that was a form of mindfulness. Mindfulness is the practice of staying in the moment, being present in your surroundings and aware of yourself. It's about acknowledging things that are both positive and negative, accepting them and letting them go.

It may sound a bit wishy-washy, but it's a psychological and behavioural philosophy based on hundreds of years of study in Eastern traditions. Mindfulness is all about encouraging yourself to see thoughts as just thoughts and your emotions as just feelings – they are what they are not a definition of who you are. Recognise them as transient mental events that come and go, rather than as aspects of your core self (i.e. intrinsic parts of your personality) or a reflection of an objective truth (you are just useless and everyone knows it). Mindfulness minimises the damage caused by bad thoughts by changing the nature of your relationship to them. It's about taking control of your mind rather than letting your mind control you – acknowledging the thought, being aware of it, but then letting it go and not dwelling on it.

According to a paper by the journal *Frontiers in Human Neuroscience*, mindfulness has been proven to give people control over their own depression and anxiety levels and it's even been shown to help with instances of chronic physical pain. Previous studies have found that it can cut the recurrence of depression by 50 per cent.

It's a meditative process that has been likened to sitting on the bank of a stream. As a leaf or a stick floats by, it enters conscious awareness. The leaf is observed, noted, and then it floats down the stream out of view. In case you didn't guess, the leaf represents your thoughts – you acknowledge them and then let them go without trying to change them, move away from them or judge them. It's a very different way of thinking and of being – but it's an exceptionally effective way of feeling happier.

⑤ Become more 'mindful'

A simple and informal way to practice mindfulness is this: be present in the moment.

All you have to do is bring your full awareness to any task you're doing or are engaged in. Anything. You could be eating, walking, driving, or getting dressed. We do so many things on autopilot we can forget ourselves in what we're doing. You need to start engaging completely with the task and employing all your senses. What can you taste, smell, feel, hear and see?

If you need help disengaging yourself from any outside interference then try the internal vocalisation approach. Say to yourself (using having a shower as an example):

> Breathe in.
> I know I'm taking a shower.
> Breathe out.
> I can feel the hot water kneading my skin.
> Breathe in.
> I can taste the water.
> Breathe out.
> I can hear it falling all around me.
> Breathe in.
> I can see swirling patterns of steam rising from around my feet.
> Breathe out.
> I can smell the scent of my shampoo.

Doing this will make you aware, physically and mentally, about what's going on now. It's very powerful and the more you practise it the less snively little thoughts like 'this isn't working' or 'have I left the oven on?' will sneak in. It's normal for your mind to drift – especially when you try it for the first few times – but then just bring your thoughts back to the present, without getting frustrated, and carry on. Don't judge yourself, just relax and concentrate hard on what you're doing. Once you become more confident at it negative thoughts will lose their power because you're not allowing them to become all-consuming.

Try this: imagine yourself on a riverbank, watching the river run past as the sun shines and sparkles on the water. You notice an oak tree over-hanging the river and as you watch a leaf falls off and drifts downwards, landing on the water and then floats away down stream. As the next leaf falls put the thought in your head onto the leaf, without getting into it or thinking about it, watch it hit the water and float away. As the next leaf falls do the same – put a thought onto the leaf and watch it land on the water and be swept away.

Yes, this may sound a bit crazy if you've never practised meditation before, but put your scepticism aside and try it for fifteen minutes every day for one week. If you really throw yourself into it and stop wondering what other people think or what the scoffing voice in the back of your head thinks it'll become easier, your mind will relax more quickly and your NATs will become less intrusive. It works.

With this informal approach you're forcing yourself to become aware of your thoughts in the moment and without even noticing, you're letting go of the stress-inducing habit of multi-tasking – assessing your thoughts while driving, eating, working. You're just being. When you've mastered this (and it takes practise) you'll be able to step outside your head and be present in the world whenever you're feeling particularly low or overwhelmed. You can become fully engaged in whatever you're doing at the time, leaving your NATs to fade into insignificance. Mindful awareness of everyday situations helps you to appreciate the richness of routine experiences, small pleasures and achievements. Things that you've been dismissing or ignoring for far too long. You could even set yourself a reminder, a phone alarm that goes off every so often nudging you to be mindful.

Of course it would be better if the NATs weren't there in the first place, which is the subject of the next chapter. However, having this strategy up your sleeve means the next time 'I'm rubbish' saunters through your head you'll be able to bat it away like an annoying fly.

Thoughts to take away

✓ When challenging your NATs ask yourself, 'What would I tell my friend?' You're much more likely to give yourself fairer advice this way

✓ Practising mindfulness will give your head a much needed break and help you appreciate the richness of routine experiences, small pleasures and achievements

✓ Thoughts are just thoughts and feelings are just feelings – they don't define you

9

Taking Charge of Your Thoughts

Now we've all agreed that negative automatic thoughts or NATs are conniving, deceitful little creeps, it's time to get rid of them. Here's how.

How to stop NATs

NATs are a bad habit, like picking your nose, cracking your knuckles or memorising all the words to awful songs. Well, actually, they're about a billion times worse than those things. NATs can affect your entire life. They can make everything seem terrible and pointless and they can make you start to hate yourself. Which is why you need to get rid of them.

Even if hideous things have happened to you, you can still change your thinking patterns about what's going on now and about what might happen to you in the future. It's never too late to feel better. And when you start thinking more positively you will feel stronger and more able to cope with everything. This will make you act more determinedly and assertively. Never forget how brave you are for trying to feel better. It's so, so hard to get the courage to face your fears. (If this were a group counselling session now would be the time for a slightly awkward back pat.)

🅢 How to stop your NATs

✦ Go back to our 'I think therefore I am' section in Chapter 8. Did you recognise any of your thinking patterns in the twelve categories listed? Yes? That's actually a good thing, because you're admitting your habit – you're addicted to thinking negatively and owning up to it will help you stop it.

✦ If you didn't recognise any of those thinking patterns in yourself then you're probably fooling yourself (or are some kind of emotional superhero). Virtually all of us, whether we're depressed or not, fall into these negative thinking traps every now and then.

You need to go back through them and be really honest with yourself. If you're still convinced that none of them adequately represent you, then ask a friend or relative which ones they would attribute to you. If you're serious about trying to feel better then you'll have to accept their opinion. Try to thank them rather than punch them.

◆ Now you've admitted it you can do something about it. Take the Golden Rules from each category that you think you fall into and really try to adopt them into your thought processes. It should be easier to recognise NATs when they pop into your head now you're looking for them. (It's like when you suddenly see a book you want to read everywhere – on posters, in reviews and being read on the bus.) Remember: these thoughts are not uninvited, you've been inviting them in. You need to kick them out pronto.

◆ If your friend told you she'd just thought something massively negative, you'd try to reassure her that she was wrong or work a way around the problem. Well, why can't you reassure yourself? What harm can there be in trying to make yourself feel better? Tell a friend your thoughts to get a balanced opinion, or, if you don't feel comfortable doing that, make yourself objective and give yourself the response you would give your friend in the same situation (as with Rach in Chapter 8).

◆ When you next think something negative, stop and assess it. Is it true?

If the answer is yes, ask yourself:
1 Does it matter?
2 What's the worst that can happen?
3 What's actually most likely to happen?
4 If that did happen could I cope?'

You'll automatically calm down because you'll realise your worst-case scenario fears are unrealistic and even if the very worst did happen you'll be able to cope with the fallout.

If the answer is no, ask yourself:
1 Why did I think it?
2 Can I recognise that I'm being unfair on myself?
3 What would I say to a friend?
4 Turn the thought on its head: 'This isn't true because …' and acknowledge and accept the proof against the thought.

If you're still struggling with the thought, you can use the strategy at the end of the chapter to really challenge it and move forward.

⑤ Thought dossier

It's essential to test and question your NATs. If you asked a salesman why the laptop he was trying to flog you was marketed as the best on the market and he replied, 'Because I think it is,' you'd dismiss him as an untrustworthy idiot. You'd want to have proof of it before you believed it, which is totally reasonable. You wouldn't just go, 'Ah, you think it is? Well, that sounds reasonable. Bag it up!'

Using negative thoughts as a crutch

Have you been thinking negatively for so long you don't even know where to start? NATs are a massive stumbling block when trying to feel happier, but things won't get better if you don't at least try to beat them. NATs enjoy hanging around, they're acting like squatters in your head and they're pretty happy about it. They're not just going to pack up and leave of their own accord. You have to kick them out.

Sometimes it's easier to take the 'If I assume the worst I'll never be disappointed' approach, but always thinking negatively about everyone and everything is extraordinarily damaging. It will affect your behaviour, your emotions and your physical health.

Humans aren't built for loneliness – we're not meant to be lone-rangers. We're social creatures. Your NATs are trying to trick you into thinking they're comforting, but they're not. Constantly thinking this way will leave you feeling isolated. Ask yourself honestly: would you rather have a negative view or a balanced view? We believe that if you're reading this book you want a balanced view, which is ace. If you take on board all the strategies you'll soon be surprised by how much better you feel and how much more positively you view life – no matter what's happened to you in the past.

> ⋯⋯ You wouldn't treat other people the way you treat yourself so why is there one rule for you and one for everyone else? You deserve to feel better, just try the strategies – really try them – and you'll notice a difference.

Checking something's validity is logical and necessary. It's the basis for all our judgements and how we all tick along in society together. The same needs to be going on inside your head. You need to start questioning these thoughts that affect you so badly.

Remember, there's always at least two sides to every story. If you did do something wrong and you did behave badly, acknowledge it and the NATs you've had about it and then qualify it. For example, if you snapped at your partner for no reason and immediately thought, 'That's just typical of me. Now he'll be in a strop about it all day and ignore me,' qualify it with the thought, 'At least I can apologise and he knows I've been having a hard time lately so I'm sure it'll be fine.'

It's imperative you get distance from your thoughts, to be able to analyse them dispassionately. Use the dossier on page 135 to note down evidence for and against an upsetting thought. Watch for times when your mood suddenly drops and ask yourself: what went through my mind just then? Catch the thought and test it.

Every time you think something negative, write it down and then fill in the blanks. It'll help you to look objectively at your thoughts and start to believe that you control them and they don't control you.

What happened	NATs	Feelings	Evidence against NAT	How I feel now
Without exaggerating, note down what honestly happened.	What thoughts went through your mind about yourself and your future? What are you thinking about others? What type of NAT is this?	What are your main feelings and emotions?	What is the evidence against this thought? What alternatives might there be? What is the evidence against this view? How would you see this if you were not feeling low? What would you say to a friend?	Write down any degree of change in the feelings you now feel.
EXAMPLE 1 My boss at work looked over my shoulder at an email I was writing moaning about her.	I'm going to get fired (the fortune teller's error). I have messed up any chance at having a good relationship with my boss (overgeneralisation/savour failure). She hates me (monochrome thinking/telepathic trickery).	Anxiety Fear Desperation	She might not have read everything I wrote. Everyone moans about their boss so if she did read it she'll probably brush it off. She might realise she's been too hard on me and back off. The likelihood of me getting fired over this is slim to none.	Calmer, less panicky, determined to work really hard and not send moany emails again.
EXAMPLE 2 I got drunk at a family party and bragged about how well my life was going.	They all thought I was arrogant or insecure (telepathic trickery). They won't invite me to the next family do (the fortune teller's error). I'll just do the same thing again through insecurity (catastrophising).	Embarrassment Shame Guilt	Everyone's behaved boorishly before. Other people were talking about their achievements. People seemed genuinely interested to hear what I'd been up to. Next time I will be calmer and more aware of what I'm doing.	More relaxed. I'm finding the whole thing quite funny. Determined to behave better next time.

What happened	NATs	Feelings	Evidence against NAT	How I feel now
EXAMPLE 3 Woke up with a sore throat the morning I had an important meeting at work	This is typical! Why do things like this always happen to me? (Why always me?) I'll mess up the meeting and won't be able to get my point across properly (fortune teller's error). Everyone will think I'm rubbish at my job (monochrome/ catastrophising)	Low Sad Defeated	I normally do well under pressure. I've got a really good track record at these kind of meetings. Just because I feel bad doesn't mean things will go badly. People will be able to tell I'm not at my best and appreciate I've made the effort to turn up well-prepared	Sometimes rubbish stuff happens – it doesn't mean life is out to get me. I know the team have a good opinion of me because of all my previous hard work

This table will hopefully show you that things aren't always as bad as you first think. You'll gradually be able to:

✦ Move from a knee-jerk reaction to conscious processing – you'll step out of autopilot.

✦ Get a change of perspective, seeing your thoughts as a passing event in the mind that's not necessarily a valid reflection of reality.

✦ Identify and question patterns of negative thinking and self-criticism. You'll feel more confident in managing your mood and become more practised at answering back your own thoughts.

✦ Turn your thoughts and therefore your emotions to more positive things.

✦ Recognise that that they are just thoughts, not facts!

How did you find filling out the dossier, did you think it was useful, hard, easy, pointless? Challenging your thoughts can take practise and may feel difficult at first; when you're low it can be hard to see things from a different perspective, especially as they often have some basis in truth. Maybe your boss did see your email, but that doesn't mean you've irrevocably damaged your relationship for good, it just means you're going to have to tread carefully for a while. If you had trusted your immediate NATs without challenging them you might have marched up and demanded to know what she'd read, putting both you and her in an awkward position. So she read your email – is it really the end of the world? If you were moaning you probably had a point and maybe she'll back off because of it or call you in to talk civilly about it. At the end of the day, who hasn't sent a ranty email to someone about their boss?

We can't stress enough how important it is to really consider these alternative thoughts and to question your doom-and-gloom predictions. When you're feeling low you fail to make a distinction between the thought and external reality – between hypothesis and fact. And, like any bad habit, it's exceptionally hard to stop doing it once it's ingrained. Beliefs about the self are ideas or opinions learned and reinforced through experience as opposed to an absolute and unchangeable truth.

⑤ Your new positive mind map

Fill in a new mind map using one of the alternative thoughts you wrote down in the dossier above. Now assess how this more positive thought affected you emotionally, physically and behaviourally. We have used the family party event as an example.

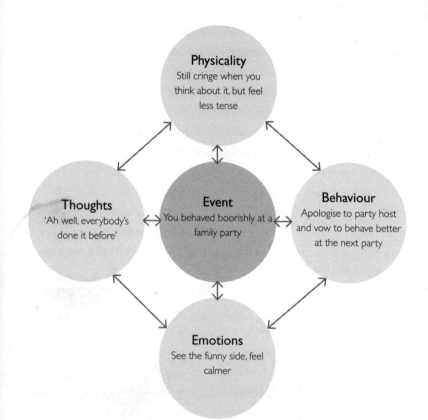

The whole thing should have a more positive bias, which is fantastic. It means you're being more realistic about things and not punishing yourself. Taking the time to assess your thoughts can make the difference between events having a terrible outcome to having a great outcome. If you'd have panicked about your behaviour at the family party, you might have avoided the next few get-togethers meaning you'd withdraw from the wider family circle, which can be a key support network. By looking at events in a different way you'll realise things aren't that bad, put on a brave face and determine to behave better next time.

Now take a moment to appreciate how brilliant it is that you've come far enough along in this process to identify your NATs, step back from them and flip them on their heads. Without wanting to break into song and dance, this is a big deal. Changing the way you think will change your life – no exaggeration. Just starting to think more realistically is a parade-worthy event. We can't throw you a parade, but we can give you a metaphorical round of applause, which we're doing right … now.

Thoughts to take away

✓ You *can* change your thinking patterns. NATs are bad habits and habits can be broken

✓ It's never too late to feel better no matter what's happened to you

✓ Every time you catch a NAT ask yourself, 'Is it true?' If it isn't dismiss it, if it is ask, 'Does it matter?' and 'What can I do about it?'

The *Real*
Meaning of Life

Finding meaning in your life and setting yourself realistic and attainable goals is guaranteed to make you feel more optimistic, positive and happy.

What happiness means to you

Don't panic, we're not going to bombard you with high-handed and pious theories on the meaning of life, but finding meaning in your life (a subtle but very important distinction) will absolutely and 100 per cent make you happy – no spiritual or religious convictions necessary.

Meaning is the last piece in the puzzle to feeling happier and the definition varies from person to person. It's an individual choice. You might find meaning in having structure and coherence to your life; you might find meaning in attaining goals or being purposeful. It doesn't matter. What does matter is the fact that people who believe their lives have meaning or purpose are happier. They enjoy greater well-being, life satisfaction and control over what they have to do and what they want to do. They feel more engaged in their work. They're more optimistic, have greater self-esteem and are generally more positive about everything. They're less anxious and they have a healthy work – life balance. Meaning acts as a buffer against psychological distress and is an integral part of maintaining your mental health.

Meaning is one of the core components of happiness.

People have searched for meaning and fulfilment in their lives since, well, forever. On a very basic level it offers a reason for living. It is what you base your core values on and it gives you a sense of direction, personal identity and social consciousness. Meaning in your life might be to raise your kids well, to inspire others, to succeed professionally or to look after your partner. There are no limits or restrictions on what drives us. But something has to or you'll feel unfulfilled and unhappy.

CBT is fundamentally concerned with meaning. The basis of the cognitive model is the concept that it is not the events themselves, but your interpretation of them that explains your reactions. It is the meaning you give these events that dictates how you act, think and feel physically and emotionally. People do not respond to the same events in the same way – the different meanings they give to the events following their appraisal is a key factor in how happy or unhappy it makes them.

These interpretations are based upon you as an individual. Your personal take will be shaped by your mood, which in turn is shaped by how fulfilled, confident and happy you feel. If you have meaning and purpose in your life we believe your interpretations of events will be more positive.

Social support

You can't choose your family – it's true. And it's also true that some people's families are full of complete lunatics. Whatever your familial situation though, social interaction with people with whom you share an emotional bond, be it relatives or friends, is essential to finding meaning. Research has proved that quality relationships give people purpose and protect against depression, while people lacking supportive relationships are at greater risk of low mood. Making time for friends and family is therefore a key part of feeling happier. However, we know this isn't always simple. If you feel lonely for whatever reason (maybe you've just come out of a relationship, moved to a different area, are having family problems, have changed jobs, etc.) then look into joining clubs to spark some social interaction. Most people sign up to classes and events to meet people just like you'd be doing. We know it's intimidating, but there are lots of people out there

Attainable goals

Another essential part of feeling happier is the pursuit and attainment of worthwhile goals. And 'worthwhile' is a key word here. The goals have to be positive and give value to your life. Striving to attain your goals and then the sense of achievement when you fulfil them, will give your life meaning.

Goals should never be about striving for perfection. Perfection doesn't exist and by accepting nothing less you'll never give yourself any credit for what you actually are achieving and will always feel as if you're failing. Instead of aiming for the impossible, aim for what is realistic for you and your situation. We're not saying you shouldn't ever aim high or try hard, but ⋯

in the same boat. Look at the website www.meetup.com/find. It's an international community of people who organise events that are open to anyone who fancies coming along. Its sole aim is to make it easy to meet new faces. Just browsing this site or signing up to one of the events or a new class will make you feel more positive as you're being proactive in making changes.

The whole point of this book is to get you doing things differently – to actually take action against your sadness, not to just think about taking action. By following the strategies we've recommended you are

⋯⋮⋅ just remember to reward yourself for doing well, rather than waiting for something that might never happen. For example, if you're an amateur actress who's appeared as an extra in a couple of regional telly shows your goal shouldn't be, 'I want to be the best actress of all time,' it should be, 'I want to get a speaking line in the next programme I'm in.' That's attainable and is something you can work towards. Being the best actress of all time isn't a measurable quantity and you're giving yourself a task you're destined to fail at because you can constantly move the goalposts i.e. 'Okay, I got my dream role, but that wasn't good enough – I need to win an award for it.'

Give yourself specific attainable goals and then reward yourself when you achieve them.

taking important steps towards feeling happier. The techniques will help towards finding meaning in your life, whether it's re-planning your week to include more things you enjoy, doing more exercise or challenging damaging NATs and seeing yourself in a more positive, and most importantly, a more *realistic* light.

⑤ Planning goals

Now that you're feeling a bit better in the here-and-now, you can start planning for the future. We want you to identify goals that you can take forward to give you a clearer sense of direction and hope, achievement and fulfilment. It's like a day-to-day 'to-do' list, but on a grander scale. You can plan both short-term, medium-term and long-term goals. Start thinking about what you want to be doing next week/month/year and how you want to be feeling. Thinking about what you want to do next and actually making the plan means you're much more likely to achieve it.

Smart goal-planning guidelines

Your goals should follow this S.M.A.R.T mnemonic: They should be

Specific

What exactly is your goal? How would things be different if you achieved it? Example: I will plan in one enjoyable activity every day for the next month to feel happier.

Measurable

It has to be something that is quantifiable so you know when you've achieved it (so not 'I will be the best actress of all time', more 'I will get a speaking part in a TV series').

Attainable

It has to be something you can realistically achieve, i.e. 'I will ask for a promotion at my next work assessment meeting' rather than 'I will definitely get a promotion at my next work assessment meeting'. Don't set yourself up for a fall.

Relevant

The goal has to be worthwhile. If you won't feel any joy or achievement in completing it then it's pointless. It has to be something that means something to you or you'll put off trying – or not bother at all.

Time-specific

Put a time on your goals. Don't just vaguely say, 'I'll do something nice next month.' For short-term goals, plan to complete them in the next month. For medium-term goals, plan for the next six months. For long-term, plan for the next one to five years.

Below are some ideas for short-term, medium-term and long-term goals taken from strategies and tools in this book that you should use as a basis to make your own staged five-year plan:

Short-term (1 month)

✦ Continue to plan in stuff I enjoy each day
✦ Make time for relaxation and to exercise
✦ Note down three good things that happen to me each day

Medium-term (6 months)

✦ Ensure I see friends and family
✦ Plan new hobbies or start old hobbies again
✦ Challenge all my NATs, so I start seeing things in a more realistic and therefore positive way
✦ Start making steps to tackling an ongoing problem in my life. (For instance if you're stuck in a miserable job or relationship start making proactive plans for how to make it better or plan an exit strategy)

Long-term (1–5 years)

+ Start a new career
+ Move house
+ Experience living abroad
+ Finish that novel I started years ago

Thoughts to take away

✓ Finding meaning in your life will make you happier

✓ Making realistic and achievable short-, medium- and long-term goals will give you an incredible sense of fulfilment

✓ Having a mix of goals – some you can achieve easily and aspirational goals for the future – will keep you motivated and inspired

A final message

Congratulations! You've read all about the hows, whats and whys of your feelings, thoughts and behaviour, have tried out our strategies and have got to the final chapter hopefully feeling more determined and happier than you did when you started.

We're crossing our fingers, toes, arms and legs that by now you're well on your way to having a far more positive outlook on life. Even if you're not skipping for joy down the road, bellowing out 'The Hills Are Alive …' you should be feeling less glum than you have done for a while – which is a big deal.

However, if you are still having difficulties and the book hasn't worked for you as well as we'd hoped, we advise you to see your GP and have a chat with them about whether you need further support. There are some useful resources and websites in the index.

But if you are feeling better – hooray! Take a moment to evaluate how far you've come and give yourself a pat on the back (or perhaps book yourself a holiday, whatever works for you). Remember, it's important to reward yourself after achieving something and feeling better – even if it's only a teeny tiny bit better – is something to be celebrated.

As a way to measure how far you've come please answer the following questions:

1 **After reading this book – how do you feel?**

   A The same – no change

   B A smidgen better – starting to think this all through

C Better – putting in place improvements

D Amazing – transformed

If you answered option A did you really invest all your energy into the strategies? Are you willing to try them again? If you did and nothing helped then we recommend you speak to your GP who should be able to recommend further treatment.

   If you answered B–D then we're very chuffed for you and things can only get better from here if you keep practising the strategies and make attainable goals to work towards in the future.

2 **Which specific skills and strategies did you find particularly helpful?** Make sure you keep practising them until they become second nature.

3 **Which of the 'takeaways' listed at the bottom of each chapter particularly struck a chord?** Write them down on a notepad or in your diary so every time you need a pick-me-up, or alternatively a kick up the arse, you can flick through and motivate yourself.

4 **What support network do you have to help you maintain what you've learned?** Consider telling family and friends what you're doing, if you haven't already. Their encouragement will be invaluable and motivational and just saying things out loud can help, giving you a bit of distance from the problem and some clarity.

5 **What possible obstacles do you see in the future that might throw you off course?** Write them down and then work through any possible solutions.

6 **Will you try to find a more balanced and realistic view of yourself and your life, remembering to look at the positives with the**

negatives and to give yourself credit for your achievements?

7 Will you stop punishing yourself for supposed 'failures' and acknowledge that 'perfection' is a dangerous myth?

8 Will you try to do and concentrate on more things that you enjoy and spend time with people who care about you?

9 Fill in the checklist of symptoms in Chapter 1 again. Have you ticked less boxes than you did the first time around?

10 When are you going to start thinking differently?

    A Today

    B Tomorrow

    C Next week

    D Next year

    E Don't care

The point of these questions isn't to harass or frighten you – they're a way of measuring how far you've come and to show you what's really going on in your own head. You have the tools to feel better – how you use them is up to you. If you're excited about making changes then we salute you. It's really hard, but hugely rewarding. And it works.

If there are some bits that you haven't managed yet, go back and re-read the chapter to remind yourself what you are meant to be doing and why. Take it a chapter at a time. You can use your success from the strategies you have managed to build your confidence and motivate yourself to take on the new ones. Some of the changes we suggest are pretty hard, so if you need more help you could perhaps ask a friend or family member to work through it with you. Just as writing things down helps, speaking about ideas and running through things out loud can really give things more clarity.

It is tough to change your behaviour and the way you think, especially as negative-biases have often been built up over years and years, but we hope you believe us that it is definitely possible. Often just starting to think or behave in a different way is the hardest bit. Actually, scrap that – just considering thinking or behaving in a different way is the hardest bit. This is why, rather than making a big song and dance about it, telling yourself you'll give it a try without putting too much pressure on yourself is a really healthy way of approaching the strategies. We want these techniques to work for you, rather than to become part of the problem. New habits take time to build and old habits can be hard to break, but they will make a real difference once you've adopted them. Make a date to re-read the book in two months or a year's time to evaluate how differently you feel next time around and to keep all the ideas fresh in your head – a kind of happiness check-up.

If you are already using all the strategies in the book then that's brilliant. Set yourself reminders about tasks on your phone over the next six months just to give yourself a nudge every now and then.

This book encourages small steps of progress, all of which add up to a big change. This isn't about waiting for the perfect job, the perfect partner, or aiming to lose a stone (those things might help of course, but only temporarily and they're hard to come by). It's about making small changes to your everyday life. If recurring thoughts, behaviours or feelings are getting in the way of what you want to do then you can challenge them using the techniques in the book. Obstacles are a part of life, but don't let them throw you off course. View them as something to be overcome and once you have you'll feel proud of yourself for having got through it. If things become very difficult again, review what you found helpful the last time and make plans to put these strategies back into practice.

Use the goals you formed in the last chapter to as a way to continue with the progress you have made. You're on your way to becoming an expert on your own mood and on how to manage during the bad times. This is all about making changes that last – that are sustainable. Of course there'll be occasions when you slip up, but these strategies and techniques will continue to work for you if you keep using them. It's about building them into your day, your week, your month, your year and about using these principles to guide you going forward so that you can feel happier.

Change can be terrifying, but everything advocated in this book is designed to help you make positive adjustments to your life. That can only be a good thing. Good luck with everything and please remember: you're not alone and you can feel happier.

Further reading

Paul Gilbert, *Overcoming Depression* (London, Constable & Robinson, 2009)

Dennis Greenberg and Christine Padesky, *Mind Over Mood: A Cognitive Treatment Manual for Clients* (New York, Guilford Press, 1995)

David Burns, *The Feeling Good Handbook* (New York, Morrow, 2000)

Gillian Butler and Tony Hope, *Manage Your Mind* (Oxford University Press, 1995)

Useful websites

MIND, The National Association for Mental Health: www.mind.org.uk

Time to Change: www.time-to-change.org.uk

Depression Alliance: www.depressionalliance.org

Be Mindful: bemindful.co.uk

Mood Gym: moodgym.anu.edu.au

Living Life to the Full: www.llttf.com

The Centre for Clinical Interventions: www.cci.health.wa.gov.au/resources

The Mental Health Foundation: www.mentalhealth.org.uk

The American Mental Health Foundation: americanmentalhealthfoundation.org

The Beck Institute: www.beckinstitute.org

Cruse Bereavement Care: www.cruse.org.uk

Relate: www.relate.org.uk/home/index.html

Frank: friendly confidential drugs advice: www.talktofrank.com

Alcohol Concern: www.alcoholconcern.org.uk

The British Psychological Society: www.bps.org.uk

The British Association for Behavioural & Cognitive Psychotherapy:
    www.babcp.com

Samaritans: www.samaritans.org

Acknowledgements

Thanks to all the people who believed in these books and helped to make them happen. Big thanks to our wonderful families, particularly Ben, Jack, Max and Edie. Also to our agent Jane Graham Maw for brilliant advice, our editor Kerry Enzor for her contagious enthusiasm and Peggy Sadler for her unsurpassed design skills. Jessamy would also like to thank the psychologists, health professionals and patients who have educated, supported and inspired her.

ALSO AVAILABLE

Learn how to combat stress, tackle anxiety
and boost energy to feel calm,
in control and fulfilled.

MANAGE STRESS
•
MAINTAIN A WORK-LIFE BALANCE
•
LEARN RELAXATION TECHNIQUES
•
BANISH WORRY AND ANXIETY
•
HANDLE PANIC
•
IMPROVE COMMUNICATION SKILLS

Quercus
www.quercusbooks.co.uk

ALSO AVAILABLE

Learn how to combat self-doubt and become more
assertive so you can succeed at whatever you
put your mind to.

DEAL WITH INSECURITY
•
NURTURE SELF-BELIEF
•
CHALLENGE YOUR INNER CRITIC
•
LEARN TO TAKE ACTION
•
PLAY TO YOUR STRENGTHS
•
LOOK THE PART

Quercus
www.quercusbooks.co.uk